The Scottish Parliament in its Own Words

an oral history

Edited by

THOMAS A.W. STEWART

on behalf of the Scottish Parliamentary Corporate Body

Luath Press Limited

EDINBURGH

www.luath.co.uk

First published 2019

ISBN: 978-1-913025-32-8 (HBK)
ISBN: 978-1-912147-97-7 (PBK)

The Scottish Parliamentary Corporate Body's right to be identified as author of this book
under the Copyright, Designs and Patents Act 1988 has been asserted.
The paper used in this book is recyclable. It is made from low chlorine pulps
produced in a low energy, low emission manner from renewable forests.

Printed and bound by
Bell & Bain Ltd, Glasgow

Typeset in 11 point Sabon by Main Point Books, Edinburgh

THOMAS A.W. STEWART began working at the Scottish Parliament in December 2017, midway through a Scottish History PHD at the University of Edinburgh, studying the political history of Dundee between the 1970s and the present day. He was originally hired as an intern on a programme supported by the Arts & Humanities Research Council through the Scottish Graduate School for Arts & Humanities, which enables organisations to access the talent of researchers to deliver a specific piece of work or project. As an intern he had a number of responsibilities, one of which included looking into establishing an oral history project that could be included as part of the Parliament's official archives at National Records of Scotland. Over the course of his internship, lasting between December 2017 and June 2018, he helped establish the Scottish Parliament Oral History Project and conducted 75 interviews with members of Parliament staff, MSPs and journalists, assembling a sizeable collection. Realising that much of this content was unique and interesting, Thomas put the idea of using the output of the project to create a book forward to key personnel within the Parliament. In September 2018, he was rehired to write this book as a member of Parliament staff, and was given almost complete autonomy to bring it together. This vision culminated in the present publication.

Contents

Acknowledgements

Many people have contributed to the successful completion of this book. I would like to thank the Information Management and Governance team at the Scottish Parliament where this author was based, and all the other members of Parliament staff who helped to bring this project together. Above all else, I give my thanks to my immediate manager during my time at the Parliament, Gordon Hobbs, without whose support, guidance and confidence, neither the oral history project nor this book would ever have started, let alone been finished. I am thankful for the Scottish Graduate School for Arts & Humanities funding for the internship that first brought me to the Scottish Parliament, during which time the bulk of the interview work was carried out. I would also like to express my gratitude to everyone who agreed to be interviewed and open up about their experiences working at the Parliament, whether as staff, politicians or journalists. This book brings together their words and is, first and foremost, their story.

Forewords

IT IS HARD to believe that it is nearly 20 years since we celebrated the opening of the Scottish Parliament in July 1999. Although that is not a long time in the history of a Parliament, a lot has happened: five general elections, landmark legislation passed, referendums on Scottish Independence and Brexit, and constitutional change. Just as significant in my view, the Parliament has become an established institution; part of everyday life in Scotland. Indeed, for anyone born after the turn of the century the Scottish Parliament has always been there – a simple fact of life.

I have had the privilege of being the Clerk to the Parliament since its establishment, to see it grow and mature. There have, of course, been many challenges, even some controversies, along the way, but that is to be expected in a fledgling political institution at the heart of an open democracy. Tough as it has been at times, it is an inescapable part of the learning process.

This book aims to capture the different experiences of those who have been at the heart of things and lived through the recent history of the Scottish Parliament. I hope you find our memories and perspectives both stimulating and informative, and a good foundation from which to contemplate the next 20 years!

Sir Paul Grice
Clerk and Chief Executive of the Scottish Parliament

THA E DUILICH a chreidsinn gu bheil faisg air 20 bliadhna bhon a dh'fhosgail Pàrlamaid na h-Alba san Iuchar 1999. Ged nach e ùine mhòr a tha sin ann an eachdraidh Pàrlamaid, tha mòran air tachairt: 5 taghadh coitcheann; reachdas cudromach air gabhail ris; reifreann air neo-eisimeileachd na h-Alba agus Brexit; agus atharrachadh bun-reachdail. A cheart cho cudromach, nam bheachd-sa, tha a' Phàrlamaid a-nis na buidheann stèidhichte; pàirt de bheatha làitheil na h-Alba. Gu dearbh, do dhuine sam bith a rugadh às dèidh toiseach na linne, chan eil àm nuair nach robh Pàrlamaid na h-Alba ann – tha i na pàirt sheasmhach de ar beatha.

'S e urram a tha air a bhith ann dhomhsa a bhith nam Chlàrc don Phàrlamaid bho thòisich i, agus gum faca mi i a' tighinn gu inbhe. Gun teagamh, tha dùbhlain air a bhith ann, connspaidean fiù, thar na slighe agus feumar dùil a bhith ri sin ann am buidheann phoilitigeach ùr aig cridhe deamocrasaidh fosgailte. Ged a bha cùisean duilich aig amannan bha e uile na phàirt den phròiseas ionnsachaidh.

Tha an leabhar seo airson cur an cèill eòlasan eadar-dhealaichte an fheadhainn a th' air a bhith aig cridhe na cùise ann an eachdraidh Pàrlamaid na h-Alba. Tha mi an dòchas gum bi ar cuimhneachain is seallaidhean inntinneach is brosnachail dhuibh agus nan deagh bhun-stèidh airson beachd a thoirt air an ath fhichead bliadhna!

Sir Paul Grice
Clàrc agus Àrd-oifigear Pàrlamaid na h-Alba

I REMEMBER HOW I felt on 6 May 1999 as vividly as if it was yesterday. My hopes, and those of my colleagues elected to our new Scottish Parliament, were boundless. It was such an honour to have been chosen by the people of Scotland to be their first representatives, and I think we all looked forward to making good on the faith we had been entrusted with. We aspired to transform this country, creating a completely new way of doing politics and building a better society.

Most of us in that first Parliament were completely new to politics, and the realities of building a new institution were undoubtedly more complicated than many had expected. We were immediately faced with a baptism of fire, with strong criticism and controversy confronting us from the start. At every moment when things have felt more settled, new events have arisen to challenge us – changes in leadership, governments and, of course, referendums. We have agonised over difficulties and celebrated great achievements. Through all this, I believe we have held firm to our sense of hope and optimism that this Parliament can make Scotland a better place. It has been a privilege to be a part of this institution over the past two decades, and observe from the inside as it has matured into such a vital and central place in Scottish public life.

As we look forward to the next 20 years, this book offers an opportunity to reflect on the Parliament's history to date. By allowing the voices of those who have worked within it to be heard, whether as politicians, staff or journalists, it will give the reader a chance to see the Parliament from a different perspective and look upon it with fresh eyes.

Rt Hon Ken Macintosh MSP
Presiding Officer of the Scottish Parliament

THA CUIMHNE AGAM mar a bha mi a' faireachdainn air 6 Cèitean 1999 dìreach cho soilleir 's gur b' ann an-dè a bha e. Bha mo dhòchas, agus dòchas mo cho-obraichean a chaidh a thaghadh don Phàrlamaid ùr Albannach againn, gun chrìoch. Abair gur e urram a bh' ann dhuinn a bhith gar taghadh mar na ciad riochdairean aig muinntir na h-Alba agus cha chreid mi nach robh sinn uile a' coimhead air adhart ris an earbsa a chuir iad annainn a fhreagradh. Bha sinn a' miannachadh mòr- atharrachadh a thoirt air an dùthaich seo, dòigh poilitigs ùr a chur an sàs agus comann sòisealta nas fheàrr a chruthachadh.

Bha a' mhòr-chuid againn sa chiad Phàrlamaid sin ùr gu poilitigs, agus bha an obair gus buidheann stèidhichte ùr a thogail gun teagamh nas toinnte na shaoil sinn an toiseach. Bha sinn air ar cur gu mòr-dhùbhlan anns a' bhad le connspaid is cronachadh bhon fhìor thoiseach. A h-uile turas a tha cùisean a' coimhead beagan nas ciùine, tha atharrachaidhean eile air nochdadh – atharrachadh ceannardais agus riaghaltais agus, gun teagamh, reifreannan. Tha sinn air a bhith a' strì ri duilgheadas agus a' dèanamh gàirdeachas ri soirbheachadh. Tro na h-uile, saoilidh mise gu bheil sinn air a bhith daingeann nar dòchas gun urrainn don Phàrlamaid seo fìor phiseach a thoirt air Alba. 'S e urram a bh' ann a bhith nam phàirt den Phàrlamaid seo thar nam fichead bliadhna a chaidh seachad, agus faicinn bhon taobh a-staigh mar a dh'fhàs i na h-àite cho cudromach aig cridhe beatha phoblach na h-Alba.

A' toirt sùil air adhart don ath fhichead bliadhna, bheir an leabhar seo cothrom meòrachadh air eachdraidh na Pàrlamaid suas gus an latha an-diugh. Le bhith a' toirt èisteachd don fheadhainn a tha air a bhith ag obair innte, ge bith an e luchd-poilitigs, luchd-obrach no luchd-naidheachd, gheibh an leughadair sealladh eadar-dhealaichte air a' Phàrlamaid agus cothrom a faicinn le sùilean ùra.

Am Fìor Urr. Ken Macintosh MSP
Oifigear-riaghlaidh Pàrlamaid na h-Alba

Chronology

1997   Referendum on Devolution. Scotland votes in favour of creating a new Scottish Parliament with tax raising powers.

1999   Scottish Parliament opens.
First Scottish Parliamentary elections.
Labour and the Liberal Democrats form a coalition government.
Donald Dewar becomes First Minister.

2000   Donald Dewar passes away.
Henry McLeish becomes First Minister.

2001   Henry McLeish resigns and is replaced by Jack McConnell.

2003   Second Scottish Parliamentary elections.
Labour–Liberal Democrat coalition re-elected with a reduced majority, small parties make significant gains.

2004   Parliament relocates from its temporary accommodation at the General Assembly Hall of the Church of Scotland to the newly constructed Holyrood building.

2007   Third Scottish Parliamentary elections.
The SNP form a minority government.
Alex Salmond becomes First Minister.

2011   Fourth Scottish Parliamentary elections.
The SNP form a majority government.

2012   Edinburgh Agreement between the Scottish and UK governments ensures that an independence referendum will be held.

2014   Independence referendum held.
        Scotland votes against independence.
        Nicola Sturgeon replaces Alex Salmond as First Minister.

2016   Fifth Scottish Parliamentary elections.
        The SNP loses its majority but remains in government.
        EU referendum held.
        The UK votes to leave the European Union.

2019   The Scottish Parliament turns 20.

Introduction

A Brief History of the Scottish Parliament

ON A SUN-BLEACHED summer's day, 1 July 1999, crowds thronged Edinburgh and dignitaries flooded into the city for the ceremonial opening of the Scottish Parliament. The moment was weighted down by history, with the presence of Scotland's ancient crown jewels and Her Majesty the Queen herself, and with inherited memories of the pre-Union Parliament that had closed its doors for the last time almost 300 years before. This was the emotional culmination of a decades-long campaign for devolution that had seen many of those present spend their political lives arguing for and against it. Yet this occasion also marked a clear departure from the past, with the creation of something completely new that was keen to emphasise its modernity at every opportunity. Indeed, the new Parliament formed one of the most significant revisions to the United Kingdom's constitution in centuries. At the same time, it was laden with the heavy expectation that it could transform Scottish politics and society in a meaningful and lasting way. This had been the promise put to Scots at the 1997 referendum, in which 74 per cent voted in favour of devolution. The institution had then been brought together in a remarkably short space of time. Less than two years separated the referendum and its first elections in May 1999, with business getting under way later that summer. In those brief months, politicians and civil servants had faced the daunting task of forging the foundations of a legislature that could live up to the nation's hopes.

The Scottish Parliament was consciously designed not to be a copy of its Mother Parliament in Westminster, which had begun to attract criticism for its confrontational style and perceived elitism. It distinguished itself in a number of key ways that it was believed would lead to the development of an open and consensus driven political culture in Scotland. The opposing benches of the House of Commons, famously separating government and opposition by a sword's length, were to be replaced by a continental European-style horseshoe shaped chamber. Committees were to be given greater influence, deference for members reduced, constricting traditions abandoned, ingenuity promoted and a more consensual, less confrontational, atmosphere encouraged throughout. One of the clearest ways in which the new Parliament departed from British political tradition was in its abandonment of first-past-the-post in favour of the semi-proportional additional member electoral system. This ensured that its political composition would be of a very different hue than Scotland's representation at Westminster had been. It allowed smaller parties to achieve unprecedented success. The 1999 poll saw the election of the United Kingdom's first ever Green Party parliamentarian in Robin Harper, alongside the 35-year-old fire-eating left-wing radical Tommy Sheridan of the Scottish Socialists. Meanwhile, larger parties like the SNP and Conservatives, who had significant popular support around the country but struggled to win in head-to-head constituency contests, were able to secure much larger groups of MSPs than of MPs. Most prominently, there was no overall majority in the chamber. Instead, the first Scottish Executive, the Parliament's new government, was made up of a coalition between the Labour and Liberal Democrat parties. This was the first two-party government elected anywhere in Britain since the Second World War.

From the start, the young Parliament was buffeted by serious difficulties. Even during the two months between its first election in May and official opening in July 1999, it had begun to attract fierce criticism and accusations of inadequacy. These voices continued to grow louder from then, with some disappointed by the slow pace of change and others angered by the policies that were being advanced. As it moved through these challenges, the Parliament was struck by tragedy. Just over a year after its inauguration, the First Minister Donald Dewar passed away following a brain haemorrhage. A lifetime advocate of devolution, Dewar had played a key role in orchestrating the Parliament's creation as Secretary of State for Scotland between 1997 and 1999, before taking over as the head of the first Scottish Executive. Although a partisan government figure, he had served as a cherished focal point of leadership for the entire Parliament. His death dealt a psychological blow to the whole institution, as it lost one of its most articulate public voices and a key source of authority. Dewar's successor as First Minister, Henry McLeish, was unable to provide stability, as he was forced to resign after just one year in office in the aftermath of an issue relating to the subletting of a constituency office. This forced the Scottish Executive to appoint a third leader in two years, with Jack McConnell elevated to the leadership. This in itself marked a milestone. Whilst Dewar and McLeish had been former MPs, with lengthy experience at Westminster before becoming MSPs, McConnell had bypassed the House of Commons entirely on his path to the Scottish Parliament. He would remain in place as First Minister for the next six years.

While these issues discomfited the Parliament, they were principally concerns of its government rather than the wider institution. In contrast, the controversy surrounding the Holyrood building project proved to be far more all-encompassing and long-lasting. When it opened in 1999, the Parliament's debating chamber was housed in temporary accommodation at the General Assembly Rooms of the Church of Scotland on The Mound, overlooking Edinburgh's Princes Street Gardens with offices scattered through the rest of the city centre. It was expected that the Parliament would be ready to uproot itself to its permanent home at a purpose-built site nestled at the foot of the Royal Mile alongside Holyrood Palace by 2001. This new building had been envisioned as an inspiring statement of the Scottish Parliament's ambition and modernity. However, it soon emerged as a lightning rod for public dissatisfaction. Many had been unenthusiastic from the start. MSPs were irked by their lack of ownership over the project, with most of the key decisions having been taken at the Scottish Office in the two years before the Parliament was opened. Both within the ranks of Scottish politicians and beyond, large numbers were concerned by the selection of the Holyrood site, with a number of alternate locations around Edinburgh having been discussed. Meanwhile the polarising modernist design of the Catalan architect Enric Miralles largely failed to excite the public's imagination, leaving many deeply unimpressed. Issues greatly escalated after work got under way on the construction. It faced a series of lengthy delays, the building finally opening a full three years after its initially proposed 2001 completion date. Miralles had died at a very early stage, just months before Donald Dewar in the summer of 2000, robbing the project of his vital direction. Most damagingly, construction costs spiralled to more than ten times the original estimate to over £400 million. While the £10 to 40 million that had first been projected during the 1997 devolution referendum was hopelessly optimistic, it set a bench mark for public expectations that were aggravated by the gradual rise of the actual costs over the years. In 2003, an official inquiry was commissioned that led to the Fraser Report in 2004 going over the numerous missteps that had been made. At times, MSPs debated discontinuing the project entirely, while it seemed that the affair risked souring attitudes towards devolution itself. Indeed, with public frustration clear to all, it appeared that the damage done by the project could be permanent. At the Parliament's lowest moments in these years, some openly wondered if devolution had a future in Scotland.

Despite the pressures put on the morale of everyone associated with the Parliament, the institution developed rapidly in these years. Captivated by an energetic and pioneering spirit, a mostly young team of staff with comparatively little experience of parliamentary traditions forged ahead with developing the legislature that had been promised to the people of Scotland. With few protocols in place, no past precedent, a need to innovate on a regular basis, and an ethos that celebrated new ways of working, individuals found the institution remarkably malleable as decisions with lasting influence had to be made frequently at a much faster and less bureaucratic rate than is typical of a large public sector body. A similar attitude was present among parliamentarians. The great majority of MSPs elected in 1999 had no prior experience of professional politics, while those raised in the political culture of Westminster were a clear minority. Many of these new politicians faced a shaky start to their parliamentary careers, confronting sharp questions over their ability relative to their colleagues in London. Yet, they soon developed a strong collegiate spirit and began to ease into their own political style as time passed.

Politically, as the Parliament came to the end of its tumultuous first session, its second election in 2003 resulted in a major shift. The two leading parties, Labour and the SNP, both suffered losses to the benefit of small parties and Independents, who flooded into the chamber. This was the so called 'Rainbow Parliament', by far the most politically diverse session since the advent of devolution. With seven Greens, six Scottish Socialists, three Independents and John Swinburne of the Senior Citizens Unity Party, taking up their seats, 13 per cent of the chamber was left under their control. The presence of such a large group of members outside the political machines of the traditional parties forced the Parliament to adapt its structures once more and make an effort to integrate them into its processes. Meanwhile, they brought a new riotous tenor to parliamentary business that had not been seen before, with the SSP in particular developing a reputation for unorthodox activity. Despite all this change, the Labour–Liberal Democrat coalition retained its majority and proceeded into its second term under Jack McConnell's enduring leadership, ensuring continuity in government even as the balance of the chamber shifted.

The most memorable event of the session occurred out with the realms of partisan politics. In 2004 the Parliament finally, and belatedly, moved into its new home at Holyrood. The building was still not loved by everyone in Scotland, but it gave the Parliament a sense of permanence it had previously lacked. Most importantly, it brought the ordeal of its construction to a definitive end. For most associated with the Parliament, and particularly those who had a hand in the building project itself, this was a relief, an opportunity to celebrate and turn a new leaf, putting the struggles of the previous five years into the past. Barring the occasional slip up, notably including a moment in 2006 when a 12-foot oak beam fell from its socket and was left dangling above the debating chamber, a sense of calm did begin to settle in. As memories of the building project began to recede in public consciousness towards the end of its first decade, the Parliament appeared to be more accepted than ever before and at ease with its own role in Scottish life.

While the institution grew more rooted, it went through a process of political change that reordered its party system. The brief flourishing of minor parties was brought to an abrupt end in 2007, with only two Greens and one Independent, the deeply respected Margo MacDonald, returning for the third session. More significantly, the Scottish Parliament experienced its first change of government. After the SNP emerged from the election as the single largest party, pipping Labour by a solitary seat, they were given the opportunity to form a minority government. In one of its first acts, it changed the name of the Scottish Executive to the Scottish Government in a symbolic assertion of authority. Regardless of its new title, the government's position was very fragile, with the SNP holding only a little over a third of the seats in the chamber and relying on the cooperation of other parties. Having grown used to operating with a government majority during the coalition years, this position renewed stress on the importance of parliamentary arithmetic and the balance between the parties. With the government struggling to cobble together the votes of enough MSPs to remain in business throughout its four-year term, it faced occasional brinkmanship, with the rejection of its budget in the spring of 2009 bringing about a spell of frantic horse-trading to avoid the need for a premature end to the session and fresh elections. This situation was then completely reversed in 2011, as the SNP won a surprise majority, the first of its kind in the Parliament's history and a feat that had widely been seen as impossible under its electoral system. Majority government put fresh strains on the Parliament's structures, that had been designed on the assumption that single-party rule would be very rare and cross-party cooperation would predominate. Some observers expressed sincere concern over the ability of MSPs and committees to provide adequate scrutiny in these circumstances, with the government able to push its policies through regardless of the views of opposition parties, and raised the danger of greater polarisation.

The rise of the SNP also led towards a referendum on the party's existential aim, Scottish independence. In the aftermath of the party's second election victory in 2011, the Edinburgh Agreement was reached between the Scottish and UK governments that gave the Scottish Parliament the power to legislate for the referendum. A date was then set for the vote in September 2014. The referendum elicited intense attention and emotions both within Scotland and across the world. As the global media descended on the country in the last days of the campaign, the Parliament was used as a backdrop – hosting journalists from far and wide in a swiftly constructed media village and becoming a symbol of the debate raging in every corner of the nation. Polling day would see the highest turnout for a national vote under universal suffrage in Scottish, and even British, history as Scots voted to stay within the United Kingdom by a margin of 55 per cent to 45. While the international media circus left after the vote was finished, the politics of the referendum remained inescapably present within the Parliament. For years, they loomed over its preceding and moulded debate. They remained central to the nation's political narrative as the country went to the polls for the next Scottish election in 2016, with the SNP government being re-elected, albeit narrowly short of a majority. This meant that it once again had to seek outside support to remain in power, particularly from the independence-supporting Greens who had secured their best result since 2003 and overtook the Liberal Democrats to become the Parliament's fourth party for the first time. There was also a momentous shift among the leading opposition parties as the Conservatives overtook Labour to become the second largest group, an outcome that would have seemed unimaginable when the Parliament was founded.

In this period, the powers of the Scottish Parliament faced their first substantial revisions since 1999. First the Calman and later the Smith commissions led to transfers of new responsibilities from Westminster to Holyrood in the 2012 and 2016 Scotland Acts. Following Britain's exit from the European Union, the Parliament's powers will be revised yet further, giving the legislature authority over ever larger parts of Scotland's governance. These new powers will undoubtedly alter the shape of the Parliament's activity as it moves into its third decade.

Through its comparatively short life, the Parliament has been concertedly tested. Its elections have delivered an array of political situations. It has seen coalitions, majority government and two very different kinds of single party minority administrations. It has witnessed passion, joy, anger and despair pass through its debating chamber and a constant churn of characters. It has lost cherished members to death, scandal and electoral defeat. It has seen patterns of work transform through technological change and at times been forced to operate under tight budgetary restraint. Through the years it has developed in both its structures and outlook, seeking to become more established while retaining the innovative spirit of a young Parliament. 1999 is deceptively distant from the present day. What was once an upstart institution, unsure of its place in the world, has now become an ingrained part of the nation's political landscape. The extent to which it has transformed Scottish politics in the manner envisioned by its founders is open to debate, yet it has undoubtedly changed them by providing a venue in which they can be discussed in greater length and detail than had ever been possible at Westminster. Across the United Kingdom, devolution is now a core facet of Britain's constitutional makeup. In 2016, many Scots born after the Parliament's foundation voted for the first time. Tens, perhaps hundreds, of thousands more had no recollection of a world without a Scottish Parliament. As this younger generation enters political life, now is an ideal moment to take stock of the Parliament's 20-year history – to investigate its origins, its early days and how it has developed over the past two decades.

The Scottish Parliament Oral History Project

The Scottish Parliament's Oral History Project (OHP) was established in early 2018 in order to capture otherwise untold memories from those working within it. This author was working at the Parliament on an internship funded by the Arts & Humanities Research Council through the Scottish Graduate School for Arts & Humanities. He was tasked by the Scottish Parliamentary Corporate Body (SPCB), the non-party political administrative side of the Parliament, to identify means by which it could improve its historical collections, and quickly took steps to begin an oral history project that would target SPCB staff and MSPs. Such a project had been considered in the past, but no action had been taken to bring it forward. With the Parliament moving towards its 20th anniversary, there was more enthusiasm for the project on this occasion and soon approval was granted to begin the first interviews in March 2018. The initial aim of the project was not to produce a publication, but to assemble a collection of recordings to enrich the Parliament's archive maintained by the National Records of Scotland. It was only after the quality of the content being assembled became clear, that the opportunity to showcase a selection of material from the OHP through this book was explored.

Oral histories seek to collect memories of the past through recorded interviews of varying length with participants in historic events. Unearthing insights and perspectives that would otherwise be forgotten by traditional written records, they have become a key resource for the research of the recent past. Projects based around parliaments and other legislatures have become increasingly common in recent years around the world from Finland to Westminster. As key seats of political power in their respective countries, the past and present of these bodies are the subject of significant public and academic interest. Finding themselves permanently in the public eye, their activities are reported on daily in the media, while they also archive large volumes of official records. Yet, even to experts, they can often appear to be impenetrable and impersonal institutions. Researchers have realised the value of historical interviews in building a more complete understanding of these centrally important institutions. They greatly enrich the historical records available both today and to future generations.

This was a particularly opportune moment to undertake an oral history project at the Scottish Parliament. It is far younger than the great majority of democratic legislatures around the world, making it possible to speak with numerous individuals who were involved at every stage of its development, from its creation up to the present day. This has allowed the OHP to examine the entire lifespan of the Parliament, constructing a more complete story of its history than is possible in more well established institutions. The Parliament's youth also provides significant practical benefits to the project. Throughout its history, it has had a very low level of employee turnover and a sizeable portion of the staff body have worked in the Parliament since its first few years, offering a rich and unexploited seam of information. This cohort will not be nearly as reachable in the future, as the larger part of it moves towards retirement in the coming years. Despite the depth of knowledge parliamentary staff possess, oral history projects of legislatures in the rest of the United Kingdom and further afield have tended not to engage with them and have instead largely focused on the experiences of parliamentarians. This places the OHP in a position to make an original contribution to the study of parliaments. It is the ambition of this project that it will bring greater attention to this dimension of political institutions, encouraging future scholars and oral historians to pay greater attention to parliamentary staff.

The project has been carried out on behalf of the SPCB. As such, it is explicitly politically neutral. However, it has not shied away from the political nature of its subject. Throughout, it has investigated the ways in which the Parliament has influenced political practise in Scotland, compared its structures to those found elsewhere in the United Kingdom and beyond, examined the political changes it has witnessed within its bounds and sought to understand how it has been shaped by them. In order to achieve this, the OHP felt it necessary to conduct interviews with current and former MSPs. While many staff are well acquainted with the Parliament's political mechanics, its elected members are most directly involved with them. Although staff have largely remained observers of the political process, members have been direct participants. Despite the inevitable electoral churn that has seen the fortunes of various parties change across the years and many stalwarts lose their seats, there remain a significant number of members who have sat in the Parliament since its first session. Similarly, many others who have left the Parliament remain, to some extent, active in public life, or were in touch with former colleagues, allowing the project to contact them without undue difficulty. As a result, the project has been able to reach many of the key political figures involved at each stage of the Parliament's history, although there are many individuals who it either failed to make contact with or did not have the time available to interview. There is an even greater imperative to reach these politicians now, than there is for members of SPCB staff. The MSPs elected in the first sessions were generally older than the staff that worked around them and, 20 years on from the Parliament's inauguration, may not be so easily accessible in the future as some retire from public life and the health of others becomes more precarious. Indeed, the death of the former Presiding Officer Alex Fergusson, who provided an enlightening interview for this project just two months before the end of his life, highlights that there is a risk that the irreplaceable recollections of individuals involved in the first years of devolution may be lost entirely if action is not taken to preserve them while they are still readily available.

As the ambition for the project grew, its scope was subsequently expanded to include a small number of press and broadcast journalists. This group is far more clearly separated from the Parliament than staff and MSPs. Yet they work intimately with the institution, even possessing offices within it. They are able to expand upon a distinct, perhaps more detached, depiction of the Parliament's history and communicate it in the vivid language of writers and broadcasters. This has aided the project in amassing a more rounded, perhaps more objective, collection of views. The Parliament's two decade long lifespan has also overlapped with a fascinating period in the history of the Scottish press, during which news reporting has been reshaped by the falling circulation of traditional printed publications and the rise of social media and the internet. The journalists involved have therefore been well placed to shed light on the changing relationship between political institutions and the media through the 21st century, a critical question for the future of democracies around the world. Although small in number, their contribution has added an important new dimension to this project.

The only key groups working at the Parliament that were left out of the project entirely were MSPs' staff and those employed in third-party contracted services. No parliamentarian in Holyrood or elsewhere would be able to cope with their heavy workloads without the aid of their staff. These individuals view the political process from an extremely close vantage point, at times engaging with the minutiae of the Parliament in greater detail than the MSPs that employ them. They are a resource that has rarely been utilised to its fullest extent by either oral history projects or other academic research. For these reasons, the prospect of pursuing interviews with MSP staffers was taken into consideration. However, there were significant concerns that would have made their inclusion in the OHP impractical. With their employment relatively insecure, there is a high rate of turnover among MSP's staff. This has meant that fewer staffers have been able to remain in their roles for a substantial portion of the Parliament's history than the participants in the three categories of individuals who were included in the project. The nature of their employment also provides additional challenges in reaching potential interviewees, who rarely possess the same public profile and easily available contact information as former politicians. This lower profile also contributed to serious difficulties in identifying suitable potential candidates to be interviewed within the short period of time the OHP had available to it.

The collection of staff involved in contracted services are far more amorphous. The Parliament awards contracts to a number of outside companies to provide a variety of services, including IT support, cleaning, catering and hospitality, building maintenance and portering. These companies in turn employ staff to carry out these roles, who work alongside the other groups within the Parliament. The perspectives from which these workers engage with the Parliament is very different to either the MSPs, SPCB staff and journalists whom this project has focused on, with their work completely separate from the parliamentary business of the institution. Furthermore, they generally come from a different social background than the other groups that were interviewed. However, the limitations in the resources of this project precluded the possibility of a significant expansion in scope. Furthermore, with comparatively few contracted staff remaining with the Parliament for lengthy periods of time, and the short period of time the OHP had available, there were notable potential difficulties in identifying suitable candidates to be interviewed. The task of approaching these groups will therefore be left to future projects to grapple with.

A total of 72 interviews were conducted over the course of the project's initial five-month run, between March and July 2018. Thirty-five of these interviews were with SPCB staff, a further 32 with politicians and five were with journalists. Five more interviews have been held since with key former MSPs and one member of SPCB staff that were not reached during the first series. This project is ongoing, and the Parliament's oral history archive will be steadily added to in the future. The interviews vary in length between 20 minutes and two hours, with most taking around one hour.

Each interview was based around a discussion of the participant's career at the Parliament, their observation of the institution, its internal workings and their opinions on its wider development. Interviews with SPCB staff were conducted according to a set script that was developed at the beginning of the project which was used as a starting point and guide for conversation. From the first, these scripts aimed to confront the more difficult moments in the Parliament's history, regardless of the discomfort this might cause the institution. The scripts used for interviews with both MSPs and journalists were adjusted to the careers of each individual beforehand. They asked a range of more political questions, but covered many of the same topics as in the staff interviews. While this meant that many very similar questions were put to all participants, every oral history interview involves a dialogue between interviewer and interviewee and the discussion within each interview varied greatly. Participants were given the opportunity to view these question scripts beforehand if they requested, but the majority of interviewees had no prior knowledge of the questions they were to be asked. All interviews were conducted by a single interviewer, who was also responsible for writing the scripts. Of these interviews, a total of 47 were chosen for inclusion within this volume. Interviews that contained unique information, or particularly evocative insights, were given preference to take up the limited space available.

This project aimed to achieve a well-rounded picture of the Parliament through its history, although it gave especial attention to its early days. This goal guided the process of identifying individuals to be invited for interviews. A different method of selection was used for each of the three categories of interviewees that were involved in this project. Members of SPCB staff were approached following the recommendations of their colleagues. Interviews were held with figures from all major business areas of the Parliament. All of these interviews were conducted on site at Holyrood, and all but one of them were with current staff. This remaining individual, Bill Thomson, continued to work closely with the Parliament from an outside role after a long career with the SPCB. While there was a preference for individuals who had been with the Parliament for a longer period, a smaller number of younger members of staff were also sought out. Participants were disproportionately drawn from higher ranking managerial roles, which often gave them a greater vantage point from which they could make broader observations, yet a number of less senior figures were also interviewed. The preponderance of these more senior individuals was in large part a result of the length of their service in the Parliament, with many having worked their way up through the ranks over the course of their time in Holyrood. The selection of MSP participants was a more delicate matter. As an SPCB project, careful attention had to be paid to ensure that members were not unduly disturbed and that the project did not favour any party or political persuasion over another. In line with these needs, effort was made to maintain a balance between the perspective of different parties, taking into account each party's relative strengths in the Parliament since the advent of devolution. This led to larger numbers of interviews with SNP and Labour members, who have together elected the majority of MSPs to have sat in the Parliament, and fewer with those from smaller parties. While the majority of interviews were conducted in the Parliament with current MSPs, a substantial number of former members were interviewed either on site or at a place of their convenience. While there was again a preference for individuals who had served for longer periods, interviews were held with current and former MSPs with a variety of levels of experience ranging from politicians entrenched in their seats since 1999 and with long ministerial careers to the youngest ever MSP, only elected in 2016. Individuals who had occupied more senior positions, or possessed unique experiences were prioritised in this selection process. Politicians were found to be very willing to be involved, with the great majority accepting invitations to participate. Media were contacted with the advice and assistance of the SPCB's Media Relations Office, and interviewed in the Parliament according to their availability. Representatives of a variety of different publications and broadcasters were invited, in order to ensure that different areas of the media were involved. However, the smaller number of these interviews in comparison to those with staff and MSPs meant that the full variety of the Scottish media landscape was not covered.

The three categories of participants produced interviews with different characters. Media trained politicians are naturally at ease expressing their thoughts and opinions. Yet oral history interviews do not have the same needs as the politicised situations they are most familiar with. There is no need for concise or cutting rhetoric and less consequence to slipping up with an ill-chosen phrase or statement. Slower self-reflection and openness are always beneficial. While the majority of MSPs had little issue in adjusting their tenor, some found it difficult to take on a more relaxed stance. In this, there was an observable difference between younger politicians, in the middle of their careers and with ambitions to rise higher, and the older figures who had reached points in their lives at which they were comfortable being open during their interviews. Although this trend was not true of all participants, it did hold for a significant portion of them. Journalists are similarly well acquainted in communicating their views and did not show a great deal of rigidity, even as they were moved to the other end of the microphone than they were used to. The approach of SPCB staff was not the same. In contrast to politicians and journalists, very few members of staff had experience of being interviewed outside of a recruitment setting, and asked to reflectively discuss their working lives for an extended period. This process therefore tasked them with moving further away from their normal experience than it did for the other two groups. More importantly, SPCB staff are strictly required to maintain their political impartiality at all times. While journalists and, to some extent, MSPs may speak freely on many or all of the political subjects asked about during the interviews, there are clear limits on what staff were able to say. This concern led to a degree of wariness around certain topics among a number of participants. However, most interviewees were able to overcome any initial caution to fully engage with the project.

While the content of all interviews were by their nature specific to the lives of each individual, a collection of shared themes and experiences emerged from the memories uncovered. They present a compelling story of the collective experience of the Parliament from the perspective of those who have worked in it. They progress from a widely felt fondness for the excited trepidation of its first years, through all the troubles, achievements and changes that followed, to a sense of confidence and stature achieved in the past decade. Yet, the interviews also pointed to the diversity of experiences within the Parliament. As would have been expected, narratives of the Parliament's history among politicians diverged greatly along partisan lines, with all developments analysed through their respective ideological prisms. More broadly, the three categories of participant, staff, MSPs and journalists, may have worked in a shared space, but have totally different objectives and day to day experiences. Consequently, they carried contrasting viewpoints into their interviews. Meanwhile, within these broader groups, individuals have engaged with the Parliament in a variety of ways. The SPCB staff are split between business facing offices who deal intimately with the political process, giving them close insights into both the mechanics of the Parliament and the characters who have been elected to serve within it over the years, and those more distant from

MSPS whose expertise lays in the wider workings of the institution that are more detached from the debating chamber. Within these two groups, they are split into an array of offices with various responsibilities through every corner of the Parliament, none of which are entirely alike. The media are separated by both the practises of their respective employers and the mediums they work in. Print, broadcasting and radio all place different demands on their journalists, and have faced diverging fortunes over the past 20 years, that has ensured that none of the participants engaged with the Parliament in exactly the same way over the course of their careers.

Despite their shared role as parliamentarians, there were a large number of divisions among the body of MSPS. Many of these divides are no different than those that would be found in legislatures around the world, between government and opposition, back and front benchers, members of smaller and larger parties, committee members and those not serving, and representatives of remote communities as opposed to members with seats near the capital, between retired members and those who are still active. All these MSPS have interacted with the Parliament and carried their work in their own ways, bringing an understanding of different aspects of the institution to their interviews. Yet, some of the divides between politicians were particular to Holyrood, or at the very least represent an innovation in historical British politics as practised in the House of Commons. Most intriguing were the ways in which list and constituency MSPS carried out their work. Following the constituency-based Westminster tradition, first-past-the-post seats are highly sought after among members and are seen as an important sign of prestige and authentic connection to local communities. Yet they are associated with a significantly heavier workload that can take over the larger part of MSPS' time. Due to the nature of political change over the Parliament's life, a significant number of interviewees had been elected to Parliament by both routes over the course of their careers, and were therefore able to provide informed insights into this aspect of Holyrood. Across the bodies of both staff and MSPS, those who joined the Parliament at its foundation, the '99ers', hold a special place. Having built the Parliament together, weaning it from birth and enduring its most testing years, they retain a special affinity for the institution and a clear bond with one another that has given their reflections a unique character throughout the project.

This volume will follow the Scottish Parliament's history in chronological order. It will be arranged as a series of extracts from the interviews undertaken by the OHP. These will be collated by theme and topic, with the author providing context to each section so that the words of the interviewees can be properly understood regardless of the reader's level of knowledge on each subject. The first section will cover the period between the 1997 devolution referendum up to the end of the first session in 2003. It will go over the establishment of the Parliament, the problems and controversies it encountered, most importantly over the building project, the pioneering spirit of the time and the new politics of devolution. The second section will carry the Parliament's story from its second election up to the end of the third session in 2011. Looking over a period when the Parliament became more firmly established, it will cover the move to Holyrood, the changing atmosphere of the period, the intriguing politics of the 'Rainbow Parliament', the first SNP minority government and the decisive 2011 election. The third section will address the years since 2011. It will provide room for recollections of the effects of a wave of budgetary restraint instituted at the start of the new decade, of the independence referendum, the politics of majority government and polarisation and the changing role of the media. The penultimate section will focus on the role of the Gaelic language within the Scottish Parliament and the reflections of the individual at the heart of its development. The final section reflects on the Parliament's journey so far. It will present five competing viewpoints on the Parliament as it reaches its 20th anniversary.

This text does not seek to be a definitive history of the Scottish Parliament. The memories it has captured might at times be unreliable. They may have been obscured by the passage of time, or been shaped by the biases, whether unconscious or conscious, of both the interviewees who described them and the interviewer whose questions they were responses to. Neither are they complete, with the project's modest resources having limited its reach, with many central figures not, as yet, having taken part. It does not aim to promote a specific viewpoint, or seek simply to celebrate the Parliament's past. It merely attempts to provide an avenue through which these stories can be brought together and provide the opportunity for the thoughts of those who have worked within this Parliament to tell their own story, in their own words.

PART I

A New Scottish Song

1997–2003

The Establishment of the Parliament

Ambitions for the Parliament

MUCH OF THE support that devolution won from voters in the 1990s, which culminated in the overwhelming endorsement of a Scottish Parliament at the 1997 devolution referendum, was not solely interested in the ideal of self-government, but was also attracted to the Home Rule movement's claim that devolution would bring about a deeper transformation of Scotland. These ideas were strongly associated with the Constitutional Convention, that had brought together Labour, the Liberal Democrats, a number of smaller parties, trade unions, churches and other civil society organisations, and produced an outline of what a Scottish Parliament would look like and what its creation would mean for the country. They promised the flourishing of a 'new politics', that would ensure that the new Parliament would not simply be a miniature House of Commons based in Edinburgh rather than London. It was to be something new, that would govern the country in a different and better way than Westminster had. It would be more attuned to the people, more modern and innovative, more representative, open, consensual and democratic. It would produce better laws, bringing about a prosperous and fairer society within a more confident nation.

Ken Macintosh, attracted to stand for the political office for the first time at the 1999 Scottish Parliamentary election, captures the optimism and boundless hope that he, many of his colleagues, and a large part of the Scottish people felt at the birth of the new Parliament.

KEN MACINTOSH, Presiding Officer and Former Labour Party MSP

My ambitions for the Parliament were far from limited, I thought we were going to transform society. I genuinely thought we were going to create a new, dynamic society in which all the wrongs of the past would be righted. We were going to put Scotland on the right path, we'd grow in confidence as a nation, put people in jobs and education, look after public services and tackle poverty. It really was a brave new dawn. I know that might sound ludicrously idealistic now, but that's what I was thinking. The list of practical policies we were going to pursue was pretty endless, but the bigger picture was where my interest lay. This idea that you could have a new form of politics, a new way of doing business, a more accessible, more consensual and discursive form of politics in Scotland, full of people with a burning sense of social justice. We had this sense of standing on the brink of history. A huge sense of destiny. We aimed to transform our world and our society.

Setting up the Parliament

While the ideas of the Constitutional Convention provided a vision of the shape of the Parliament, the practical process of creating a new legislature proved far more complex and detailed than the blueprints the Convention had provided. This task was left to a small group of politicians, and civil and public servants, to carry out in an extraordinary short period of time. Just 26 months separated the election of a Labour government committed to enacting devolution in May 1997 and the formal transfer of the power to legislate on Scottish affairs from the British to the Scottish Parliament in July 1999. The gap between the referendum in September 1997, in which the Scottish public gave their endorsement to devolution, and the first elections to the new Parliament in May 1999 was even shorter. During that time, the details of the devolved settlement were formally decided, a swathe of complicated legislation was passed through Westminster and the structures of a brand new institution were put in place. The creation of a new Parliament or legislature is a very rare occurrence. For it to take place in such a brief period, outside of the context of war or revolution, was even more remarkable.

Individuals closely involved with this process discuss how this was achieved. Henry McLeish, then Minister of State for Scotland – effectively the second ranking politician in the Scottish Office, and Wendy Alexander, a close advisor to the Secretary of State for Scotland Donald Dewar at the time, observe the political side of the process, while Paul Grice and Andrew Mylne comment from the perspective of the civil and public service.

HENRY MCLEISH, Former Labour Party MSP, Scottish Labour Leader and First Minister

For those of us who had laboured away for years under Conservative governments, Labour's victory in the 1997 election was a glorious moment. This was an opportunity for Wales, Northern Ireland and Scotland to figure. But it was also about significant sentiment. Because our former leader John Smith had died before he could see the Scottish Parliament become a reality. He left a legacy, saying that this was Scotland's unfinished business. Tony Blair approached this with great enthusiasm, supported by Gordon Brown, and of course the main architect of the operation Donald Dewar. So, in 1997, we prepared the White Paper very quickly. It was designed to do two things. One was to outline to Scotland what the thinking was and seek their support. But it was also tactically to make sure that once the issue got into the House of Commons we wouldn't have so many problems. Because if people were able to vote in the referendum on the White Paper, then that would help us ease the legislation through Westminster. It was all part of a kind of grand strategy. That had much to do with the wisdom of Donald Dewar and his vision.

There were significant personal pressures involved in getting the Parliament set up, but there was also a powerful political high. This was history. Substantial powers were being given to Scotland for the first time since 1707. We were emboldened by the fact we were going to have a statute with a Scotland Act and a reopening of the Scottish Parliament. They were exciting times, but it was hard work. People forget that even after the White Paper was published, there were those at Westminster, including some of the big beasts, that wanted to dilute what we had achieved. The trio of Donald Dewar, Gordon Brown and Tony Blair made sure that didn't happen. Donald Dewar emerged with enormous stature because he had to fight these bitter battles in parliamentary committees and cabinet committees, but he won through.

As Minister of State, the number two at the Scottish Office, I dealt with the detailed nuts and bolts of the Bill and took it through the floor of the House of Commons. I did 120 hours at the dispatch box to make sure the legislation went through. I often joke that within the parliamentary passage the person who gave me the toughest time was the late Tam Dalyell, a fellow Labour MP who had a conviction that this was not good for Scotland. Every day when I was there in committee, sitting a few feet away from my right-hand shoulder was the Honourable Member. He was really the most interesting, erudite and best informed of the critics that we got on the floor of the House. Of course, in the end the Bill got through and the Scotland Act was signed.

There was never a great fear that things were being too rushed. Partly because a lot of the work had been done before we even reached government. Once we had gotten into the 1990s there was a growing mood in favour of devolution in Scotland, the Constitutional Convention had brought people together and produced ideas, Labour had commitments in our manifesto. The pathway was identified, and we walked quickly through it. There weren't really any fears.

WENDY ALEXANDER, Former Labour Party MSP and Scottish Labour Leader

Labour won the election on 1 May 1997, Donald Dewar was appointed Scottish Secretary on 2 May, and by 4 May we were in St Andrew's House being briefed on the devolution legislation that the Scottish Office had worked on. They had done a very good job, because unlike previous attempts at having Scotland Acts in the 1970s, which had been read by the Cabinet Office, it had been agreed that the Scottish Office would have a leading role. We'd taken that very seriously and put the best team on it. So, when Donald arrived in office, there was a thick ring binder ready for him saying, 'Welcome minister, here are the 30 decisions you need to take'. I think Donald enjoyed being involved in that process.

But due to Labour's manifesto commitment to holding a referendum, it quickly became apparent that there was an incredibly tight timetable to publish a White Paper on which the people could vote on in the September of that year. To have people vote, we needed to have a Referendum Bill. The peculiarity of the Westminster timetable meant that the White Paper should be agreed by 25 June, published on 25 or 26 July. There then had to be an elapse of time to allow the referendum to take place in September. There also had to be parliamentary time set aside to get the Referendum Bill made. What that meant, was that Donald was working flat out, he had less than six weeks to agree and negotiate support for all the essentials of the new Scotland and Wales Act, the terms of the Scotland Act, the terms of the White Paper and of the referendum. When you look at how the subsequent referendums, whether on Brexit or independence, were handled, it was a phenomenally short time span. There was absolute focus for those first few months.

The assumption in the Scottish media had been that the Constitutional Convention had decided everything already. But there were lots of things that the Convention hadn't resolved or thought about. The form of the Act, how to deal with reserved issues, the role of the Monarchy, the detail of the relationship with Europe, the boundaries of Equalities legislation, and much else besides, had to be decided. There was quite a lot of unfinished business. To deal with these questions, there was a huge amount of negotiation inside Government. Donald was very respectful of Cabinet government, so he didn't come out every minute to brief *The Herald* and *The Scotsman* on what was happening behind closed doors. But a lot of battles had to be fought and refought. There were issues that had to be explored, that some people were exploring for the first time, because the Convention had been a Scotland-only process that those in the rest of the UK hadn't been engaged with.

PAUL GRICE, SPCB Clerk and Chief Executive

I was in the senior civil service at the Scottish Office and in the run-up to the 1997 election we looked at party manifestos. At the time a Scottish Parliament was a major plank of the Labour Party manifesto. If they were elected, they would pursue devolution for Scotland and a referendum. I was told that in that event, I would be one of the three group heads forming a Constitution Group to take that forward. So, I and with a number of colleagues worked on the White Paper of what that legislation would look like and what the referendum might look like. As it turned out, Labour did win, Tony Blair became Prime Minister, Donald Dewar was made Secretary of State for Scotland. I was very fortunate that I was part of that. My first responsibility was to look after the legislation for the 1997 referendum, and then take responsibility for the founding legislation in 1998. When that was nearly done I was told that I was going to be made Director of Implementation to actually establish the Parliament. It was a fantastic opportunity. From about the autumn of 1998, I moved away from the Constitution Group and formed my own group, and set about establishing The Parliamentary Service. My first focus was on the temporary accommodation, I wasn't responsible for the Holyrood building at that point. The goal was to make sure that we had a Parliament, a functioning Parliament, by the 1999 elections.

Looking back, there was a sort of naïvety that helped us in establishing the Parliament in such a short period of time. It never occurred to us that we couldn't do it. There was a terrific sense of optimism. We had an absolute deadline, the elections were going to be held on the first Thursday of May 1999, and that was certain. Training helped. I remember when I was in the senior civil service, I went off to do a training course and as a part of it I spent a day at a Honda car plant. The man that ran that was an inspirational guy. His office was lined with this chart, showing all the project timelines to the opening of this new state of the art factory. It was an immensely complicated thing. I remember asking him what happens if he didn't hit his deadline, and he just looked at me and said, 'We will hit our deadline. It's not whether you hit it, it's about what you have to do to make sure you do' and I was always inspired by that spirit.

So, I adopted that approach at one level, a quite onerous project management approach, we had very detailed timelines on everything. I understood that we had to have some good planning, so I made sure I had people around me who were good at that. We looked at other parliaments very rapidly, New Zealand, Sweden, Ireland, obviously Westminster. I quickly recruited 60 to 70 outstanding people who were fantastically well-motivated. We had the great benefit of blueprints developed by the Constitutional Convention and a cross-party group chaired by Henry McLeish, the Consultative Steering Group, or CSG. Those were immensely helpful, we didn't have a blank piece of paper, we had things to work on. There was just an absolute sense of mission, purpose and focus, with tremendous political support from people like Donald Dewar and Henry McLeish when we needed it. I never once had to tell anyone to work hard, my job was just to try to direct them. That's how we did it.

ANDREW MYLNE, SPCB Clerk Team Leader

I joined a number of months before the Parliament was first elected and first met. The focus at the beginning was to put in place the bare minimum procedures that we thought we would need for those first few months. It was an enormous achievement for a relatively small group of people. We put in place a set of procedures and working practices and an ethos. We got to a position where the MSPs essentially trusted us. When we gave them advice and steered them in a particular direction, they would go with us. All of that was put in place in a relatively short period of time.

The first phase was just working out what all of that was going to look like, and put flesh on the bones that had been given to us in the Scotland Act and the Consultative Steering Group report. Some of that involved working with Scottish Office solicitors in finalising a statutory instrument which contained all the initial standing orders of the Parliament. That was a huge job. But a lot more of it was just sitting down with colleagues and asking, 'What is a committee meeting going to look like? What sort of papers are we going to produce? How do we write minutes? How are we going to organise our filing system?' All that needed to be put in place. By and large, everything worked and nothing fell badly over in that first six months to a year after the Parliament had opened. Some of those early committee meetings would look pretty clunky if you looked back now, and some of the practices might seem a bit odd. But they essentially worked.

Over the rest of session one you can see that phase of bedding in continue, where lots of things were being done for the first time, or the second or the third. Quite quickly, people started to realise where things didn't work as well as they would like and what needed to change. But I think if you look at the original standing orders, as they were put in place by a statutory instrument in 1999, and look at them now you will see that there is a remarkable continuity. I would say roughly two thirds of it is essentially as it was in 1999. The basic structure and the basic concepts are still largely the same in most areas. I think that shows how much we got right in the first phase.

Being Different to Westminster

The mandate to create this new form of politics led to an explicit rejection of the institutions, procedures and political culture of Westminster. These demands were given concrete form in the report of the Consultative Steering Group, or CSG, that published a set of proposals on how the Parliament should operate in December 1998. These ideas acted as a guide for the civil servants, and later SPCB staff, tasked with developing the new Parliament and quickly became central to their thinking.
David McGill admits that these ideas often crystallised into a reflexive anti-Westminster sentiment, that at times rejected London's way of doing things with little consideration.

DAVID MCGILL, SPCB Assistant Chief Executive
Our biggest check when designing our practices was Westminster. What Westminster did and how it did it. Quite often we would look at how

they did things in London, and make a conscious decision to do something else. One of the reasons for the levels of excitement and motivation around the Parliament was that it was going to be different. It was going to be more open and progressive. This goal was something that staff were definitely aware of and were committed to. We all knew about the CSG report, it was probably something that we had all sat and read. We just dismissed Westminster as being very closed, very traditional, very hidebound by that tradition. Whatever they had done, had to be wrong in our book. We had to do things the modern way, the right way. I think with hindsight we downplayed the value of tradition. When some of our staff travelled down to Westminster to speak with our opposite numbers, and really properly look at how things were done there, we could see how things had built up over time and could appreciate it more. I'm not sure we went as far as cutting off our noses to spite our face, but I think we could have given more cadence to how things had evolved at Westminster over hundreds of years, rather than just completely dismissing it out of hand.

The First Days of a New Parliament

The Birth of the Parliament

The Scottish Parliament was born over the spring and summer of 1999. After months of preparation, elections were held on 6 May 1999. The new MSPs then assembled in the chamber for the first time on 12 May, where the eldest member Winnie Ewing proclaimed that, 'The Scottish Parliament, adjourned on the 25th day of March in the year 1707, is hereby reconvened'. However, the Parliament was not formally endowed with the power to legislate until 1 July, following a grand opening ceremony.

The Clerk and Chief Executive Paul Grice looks back to his eagerness for the Parliament to make a good first impression on the newly elected members on the morning after that election. Ken Hughes turns to the Parliament's first sitting and an awkward clash between untested protocols and reality, that captured much of the spirit of those sometimes ramshackle first months in a single moment. Finally, the Labour MSP Iain

Gray and Douglas Millar, then a young man working in one of his first jobs as an SPCB administrative assistant fondly remember the excitement and celebration that accompanied the formal opening ceremony.

PAUL GRICE, SPCB Clerk and Chief Executive

I was sweaty palmed on the morning after the first election. People had said that after the election it would take days or weeks before anyone started to wander in. I said, 'No, we had to be there at seven o'clock the morning after the election. If I was a member elected to this new Scottish Parliament then I would want to be able to come straight from the count, walk in the door and have someone there to receive me'. One or two members did come in that next day, even though most didn't stop by until later. I wrote a personal letter to every newly elected member to be delivered by hand on the Friday after the election saying, 'Welcome, congratulations on being elected to the Scottish Parliament'. You had guys on bikes and cars delivering these throughout Scotland, because I wanted them to feel immediately special. It was a nice way of creating a good impression early on. Under the water there were feet thrashing around like mad, but on the surface, I wanted the new members to walk in to what appeared to be a fully functioning Parliament waiting for them.

KEN HUGHES, SPCB Assistant Chief Executive

I have strong memories of the first day of the Parliament, 12 May 1999. Not to indulge in hyperbole, but there was international interest in this historic day for Scotland. I was involved in a lot of work in setting up that first meeting of Parliament where we had to swear all the members in. One of my duties that day was to carry the ballot box to Winnie Ewing, she was sitting in the chair as the oldest member. The first function after swearing in was to elect the first Presiding Officer. In our wisdom, we had decided that whoever the chair was would be able to vote in that election by getting out of their seat and going to the ballot box. But we had already decided that if the chair got out of their seat then the meeting was suspended. How were we going to solve this one? Our solution was for me to carry the ballot box over to Winnie Ewing and haul it over the desk so she could cast her vote. As I lifted the box the flap that the ballots were placed in closed over, and she couldn't get her vote in. I remember worrying that this was on the television, it was risking turning into a farce! But we resolved it eventually, and things proceeded from there.

IAIN GRAY, Labour Party MSP and Former Scottish Labour Leader

It's hard to remember the sense of excitement and optimism. We were the first members of the new Scottish Parliament, it felt like being part of history. There was an enormous amount of goodwill for the Parliament from the Scottish public, certainly in those first days. I remember during the opening ceremony there was a parade of children from schools all around the country, and while we watched it one of my fellow MSPs turned to me to say that this was the best day of his life. It was fantastic, the day could not get better. Just as he said that, Concorde and the Red Arrows flew over our heads, and he just burst into tears. That is what it was like. It was just so wonderful. That day was wonderful, even if that feeling quickly dissipated afterwards.

DOUGLAS MILLAR, SPCB Events Manager

I remember the opening ceremony. I was based on the first floor of the Lothian chambers building, which was on the Royal Mile next to St Giles' Cathedral. We were watching the ceremony on the TV, and when the march came up the Royal Mile towards us we would open the windows and sit on this large concrete decoration hanging over into the street. Sean Connery was leading the march. He was waving to everybody and looking around, when he looked over to our building he saw me and pointed out to say, 'Don't jump!' Which made us all laugh. Later on during the celebration, myself and some of my colleagues managed to get up onto the roof, it was more of a scramble onto the roof if I am honest. But when we were up there we couldn't see anything, because St Giles' was in the way. And then, you heard this almighty roar as Concorde and the Red Arrows flew right over our heads. None of us knew that was going to happen. That moment gave me goose pimples through my body, my ears stood on end. It was fantastic.

The Early Days Spirit

Despite the great challenges they faced in this period, a large portion of the staff and politicians working in the Parliament in its first days maintain fond memories of the spirit that surrounded it at that time. They felt a strong camaraderie with the rest of the Parliament, and equally importantly enjoyed the excitement of being pioneers with the power to mould a new and evolving institution on a daily basis. This was a singular moment when individuals across the Parliament had the freedom to work through problems and bring about real change, without the constraints of bureaucratic deliberation that slow down most large organisations, holding them back. Once the Parliament had become more settled, the same feelings of innovation and togetherness couldn't be preserved in the same way.

Fiona Hyslop and Ruth Connelly celebrate the positivity and unity of the Parliament in this period, speaking for members and staff respectively. Stephen Imrie and Andrew Mylne then describe the satisfaction they gained from the feeling of adventures that the opportunities available within a new Parliament presented, a situation that contrasted with their previous experience working in parliaments elsewhere. However, Douglas Millar warns that some of the retrospective warmth for this period of the Parliament's history may be coated in nostalgia, as he recalls the instability of a time in which large numbers of staff chose to leave the Parliament at the earliest opportunity.

FIONA HYSLOP, Scottish National Party MSP

Everybody was under a lot of pressure, but there was a huge enthusiasm, everybody was happy to be there. Across parties, we supported each other as individuals, even as there was obviously always party politics in the chamber. The staff were a part of it too, they were always very friendly and approachable, I think everybody felt they were in it together, right from the start. Whether they were an MSP or whether they were a member of MSP staff, part of the security team, part of the catering team, or part of the Official Report, it did feel as if we were part of one big moment together. It was the first Parliament we'd had for hundreds of years. I think people would really feel part of the Parliament collectively and as a sense of loyalty to it.

RUTH CONNELLY, SPCB Head of Broadcasting

I felt hugely privileged that I was going to be there, in at the beginning of the Parliament. There was a great sense of camaraderie among every office. It was a close-knit group, who were working really hard and sometimes going above and beyond the call of duty in terms of the hours and effort we were putting in. Everybody was working towards this one goal, of getting the Parliament up and running, and all of us were working really hard to get it there. There was a real sense of achieving something on a daily and a weekly basis, as we were putting together these offices and their remits. I'm coming up to retirement now, and all my working career, this was the high point. Even today, being able to say you were a part of that original staff group is a badge of honour that we take pride in. It feels a bit like being in an exclusive club.

STEPHEN IMRIE, SPCB Clerk to the Justice Committee

After working at the European Parliament, the best thing about the Scottish Parliament was that we were smaller and we were new. That's my abiding memory of the early days. The newness of everything that you did. There was nothing written down on paper that showed you how you were supposed to do it, there was no one really to talk to who could explain things and there were no guidelines. So, you had to think on your feet. That was the best bit of the early days. It was quite thrilling and quite a challenge. It made you think, and probably make some mistakes along the way, but it was liberating. You really had to take everything back to first principles. What's the best way of doing this? How should we go about doing it? We had the founding principles of the Parliament, but we had fresh new challenges that you had to work out every day. It was quite exciting really.

ANDREW MYLNE, SPCB Clerk Team Leader

It was an ideal opportunity to get in at the beginning of a new institution that wasn't held back by centuries of tradition, where everything had to be done in a particular way because that's how it had always been done. There was a strong political consensus that the new Scottish Parliament would be different, and was to break the mould from Westminster. This was not just about creating a mini-Westminster in Scotland that would bring decision making closer to the people, it was also about trying to do things in a newer, more modern and less pompous way.

Being a part of it was a very different experience to working at Westminster. When you were in a clerking role there, you mostly processed bits of parliamentary business that people brought you that particular day, or that particular week. You didn't often get the chance to step back from that day to day stuff and ask, 'Are we doing this the right way? Is there a better way of dealing with legislation or getting the committees to do their work? Should we try something really different?' You very rarely get to do that when you are working in a traditional parliamentary context. The satisfying thing for myself and others who worked in the Scottish Parliament, particularly in the first two sessions, was the ability to really radically rethink things and try out different approaches. When you work in institutions that are long-standing and have the inflexibility that comes with age, you can't do that. It's not about how tremendously wonderful or clever or perceptive we were, it was more a case of being in the right place at the right time. That was very satisfying to be a part of.

DOUGLAS MILLAR, SPCB Events Manager

I saw a lot of staff leave in a very short space of time in the first months of the Parliament. We had taken on a lot of the staff from the Scottish Office. I understood that they had a period where they could decide if they wanted to stay with the Parliament or if they wanted to go back. I think nearly everybody who had that choice went back. I remember people coming in and thinking, 'Oh no, this is not done. I don't like this'. I think it was maybe a bit chaotic for them, it was perhaps out of their comfort zone, they didn't like the way the Parliament was working. If you had come from the Scottish Office, where everything is very well structured, and you had been there for years and years, you would have thought that this organisation was a bit all over the place, a bit of a mess. My job as an administrative assistant was very straightforward, I had no problems. But a lot of the people above me in management left. I remember that first Christmas we received a £100 bonus. I took it as a thank you for still being here. I think they knew the value of those who had stuck with them.

Parliament Standards

By the end of the 1990s, concerns over Westminster 'sleaze', the malpractice of politicians, had grown particularly acute in the public consciousness after a series of damaging scandals. As a part of their central desire to achieve a better form of politics under devolution, the architects of the Scottish Parliament were eager to disassociate the new institution from these problems and promote a cleaner public image. There was therefore a determination from the first to introduce stronger rules and parliamentary standards that would ensure that MSPs behaved more appropriately than their counterparts had in Westminster.

As the first Convener of the Standards Committee, Mike Rumbles played a part in establishing these protocols. He recalls how he came into this position, and the first actions he pursued in his new role.

MIKE RUMBLES, Liberal Democrat MSP

In 1999, the rest of the Liberal Democrat group who weren't ministers were allocated committees. Jim Wallace asked, 'Who would like to be convener of the Standards Committee?' It was like the old joke about the army lining up and someone saying, 'All volunteers step forward' and everyone takes one step back. So, I thought if nobody else wanted to do it, then I would do it. I thought it was a job that I could do, and a chance to see if we had any skeletons in the cupboard. The Standards Committee is very important, there had been so many scandals in the House of Commons – 'cash for questions' among others. I wanted to make sure that we set off the Parliament in the right way, so I took on that role as convener of the Standards Committee.

Then it was a baptism of fire with the first scandal of the Parliament, which was allegations of access to the Finance Minister that the press dubbed 'Lobbygate'. This scandal broke in the September, and Jack McConnell was Finance Minister at the time, it was the Saturday night and the *Observer* was about to break the story the following morning. Jack McConnell rung me up in the middle of the night and asked me to investigate what had happened. Being a new committee at the time, we didn't have any rules to follow, so we had to investigate this ourselves. What this made clear to me was that we needed an independent process. It was wrong for an MSP to investigate another MSP. I was quite clear that we had to establish an independent Standards Commissioner. That turned out to be the first Committee Bill of the Parliament, I took that through with the committee members, and we established this independent commissioner and that got us on the right foot.

Women's Representation

One of the most visible ways in which the politics of the Scottish Parliament distinguished themselves from Westminster was in the representation of women. At its foundation, the Scottish Parliament had one of the highest levels of female representation of any legislature in the world, with women occupying 37 per cent of parliamentary seats. This was partly achieved through a controversial twinning policy adopted by Labour, by far Scotland's leading party at the time, that led to the party achieving a remarkably even gender balance. Although not adopting the same formal mechanism, the other parties also elected substantial numbers of female MSPs. This meant that women made up twice as large a proportion of the Scottish Parliament as they did the House of Commons. At the time, just 18 per cent of MPs were women, with half of those members having been freshly elected in 1997 and consequently occupying junior roles. This gap has subsequently closed. In Edinburgh, women's representation fell modestly from its 1999 peak, although never dipping below a third of MSPs, while the situation in Westminster has greatly improved over the years. Yet in 1999, the two Parliament's appeared starkly different.

Three of the women elected in that first cohort, Jackie Baillie and Wendy Alexander of the Labour Party and Fiona Hyslop of the Scottish National Party, reflect on the decisions that led to that level of representation, and the way in which it shaped the Parliament from its early days.

JACKIE BAILLIE, Labour Party MSP

The Labour Party had decided to do things very differently for the 1999 election. The culture used to be that you decided in smoked-filled rooms who the favourite son was, and he would be the candidate. We argued long and hard prior to the first Scottish Parliament election that Labour should adopt a more professional way of doing things, but that its approach should also be underpinned by a gender mechanism – twinning. So, at the very start of the process we had to fill out an application, as you would for any job, and you would make it onto a shortlist. We were then interviewed by a large panel, I had great fun at it as I didn't take it that seriously, so they whittled down however many hundred applicants to a short list of 200. Constituencies were twinned together to make sure they picked a man and a woman in each, with one having an all female shortlist to choose from. The twinned constituencies were very similar in terms of their demographics and the likely outcome of the vote there, so we made sure that there were equal numbers of men and women standing in winnable seats.

WENDY ALEXANDER, Former Labour Party MSP and Scottish Labour Leader

The Constitutional Convention had a commitment towards 50/50 representation of men and women in the Scottish Parliament. We got a lot of advice from the Law Officers, that was confidential and couldn't be shared at the time, about whether it would be legal to compel parties in an Act to have 50 per cent representation. Donald Dewar felt it was something that we couldn't do. But, true to the spirit of the Convention scheme, the Labour Party committed itself to select equal numbers of men and women for the first devolved election in 1999 through a mechanism called pairing. It was an extraordinary opportunity, because you had a clean slate. At that point, I thought, 'Goodness me! I've spent all this time writing about devolution, I've been an advisor on it, wouldn't it be fun to be a woman in the first cohort of the Scottish Parliament'. So, I went back to Renfrewshire and became the candidate for Paisley North, going through a female only selection system, and was elected. To this day, it's a very good way of achieving equal representation. That shaped the character of the Parliament. If you have over 30 per cent women, as the initial Parliament did, it's never going to have the exclusive character of a boys' club. It is something that Scotland and those parties who upheld it can be proud of.

FIONA HYSLOP, Scottish National Party MSP

I think the number of women in the Parliament right from the start helped shape its character. We were never ever going to be an old boys' club, and I don't think we've lapsed into that since. I think there was an element of mutual respect, that women were not patronised in the way that they were in Westminster, and that the issues that affected women were put up front right from the start. I don't think, for example, that health was an issue ever given the high profile at Westminster that it very clearly had here in the Scottish Parliament. I think that's a lot to do with the fact a lot of women work in the health service and it's an issue that women always rate very highly in terms of their interest. On top of that, one of the first debates we had in the Parliament was about domestic abuse. I remember thinking in that moment, 'Oh my goodness, this is how things have changed'. That would never have been a priority for debate in Westminster. The difference it made to the style and subject matter were evident from the start.

A Steep Learning Curve

Just as the Parliament itself was new, and its procedures untested, the majority of the members elected to sit in it were entering professional politics for the first time in their lives. Ninety per cent of them had never served at Westminster. A seem of inexperience ran right through the chamber. As they tried to learn what it meant to be parliamentarians, within an institution that was still in flux, and with the burden of heavy public expectations on their shoulders, many struggled. Some fell short of the standards elected members are held to. Speeches were poor, ideas unimaginative and dealings with the media naïve. For many, the learning curve was simply too steep.

Former First Minister Jack McConnell describes the three main groups of members, those coming from Westminster, those with extensive non-parliamentary political experience, and those totally new to professional politics. The Labour MSP Johann Lamont, recalls her memories of being thrust forward as one of the political newcomers elected in 1999. Dennis Canavan, a veteran operator who had spent a quarter-century in the House of Commons, admits his disappointment at the calibre of some of his fellow MSPs in those first years. The SNP's Alex Neil makes the important point that it was not solely the new parliamentarians who lacked experience in their new roles. The party leaders, most of whom were seasoned by years in Westminster, were themselves being asked to take on the responsibilities of leadership positions on a different scale than they had ever held before. For all their know-how, they too were learning on the job.

JACK MCCONNELL, Former Labour Party MSP, Scottish Labour Leader and First Minister

In the new Parliament you had three kinds of members. At one end of the spectrum, you had experienced Westminster parliamentarians, from all parties, who had returned to Edinburgh and were committed to the new Parliament. I think they found the transition very hard. They were used to a relatively secluded lifestyle in Westminster. There wasn't the sort of day-to-day pressure of attention, especially on backbenchers, that we ended up getting quite quickly in the Scottish Parliament. They certainly weren't used to serving in a Parliament that didn't have a majority for one party.

The second group was made up of people who were complete newcomers to politics. They were very inexperienced in terms of parliamentary procedures and weren't used to exercising their judgement in that context. That was not to say that they were not making a contribution, but they had a different level of experience.

The third group was in the middle. It was made up of people, like myself, who had significant local, and sometimes national, political experience, but had never been a Member of Parliament before. From that group, there was quite a number of us who were immediately thrown into ministerial office. It was a strange and challenging experience. It was very immediate. While there had been a lot of work done to prepare the Scottish Executive and the Parliament for their establishment, everybody, the civil service, the support staff, the media, external organisations and the members, were to some extent feeling their way forward.

JOHANN LAMONT, Labour Party MSP and Former Scottish Labour Leader

We were on a learning curve really. I think that in the chamber itself, we were all testing what it meant to be a politician. I'm sure that if you look back at some of the debates they will not be very sophisticated and they will maybe be a bit shouty. When everything is new, there is nowhere to hide. If somebody goes to Westminster and they don't know what to do, you'll be told very quickly, 'Well you don't do it that way and that's a tradition'. Whereas, if somebody said to us, 'Don't do it that way', we'd say, 'Why? Why do we not do it that way?' You couldn't presume a way of conducting yourself. It took a while to bed down. In fact, one of our colleagues elected in 1999, Ian Welsh, resigned very early on. That in itself was a big shock for everybody. I think that the Parliament wasn't where he wanted to be and wasn't what he wanted it to be. That early stage was very unsettling for a lot of people, there was a lot of anxiety. The institution needed to be given time to bed in, but we didn't have much time.

DENNIS CANAVAN, Former Independent MSP

The standard of debate in the Scottish Parliament was not as good as in the House of Commons at first. There were a lot more experienced politicians and polished performers at Westminster who could take part in debates. In contrast, the Scottish Parliament was rather unexciting. There was little of value in the daily speeches, very little interchange of ideas and few new ones. A lot of the MSPs, especially new ones, were simply getting up and then reading a speech that had been written for them by some party hacks. Some of them couldn't even read out the speeches very well. At first, I wondered what on earth I had come into. I do think that with a bit more experience, most of the MSPs improved. Certainly, over the years the standard of debating has improved from where it was at the beginning.

ALEX NEIL, Scottish National Party MSP

None of the party leaders in the first session had ever led a large parliamentary group before. Donald Dewar had never been a leader of a party, so he was new to that kind of leadership. Although Alex Salmond had by then been leader of the SNP for nine years, he had never led a parliamentary group of 35 people, some of whom he didn't know all that well. At Westminster, he had a been leading a very small group of people. David McLetchie of the Tories had never been an elected representative, let alone a party leader. Jim Wallace had never been a party leader either, and at that time the Lib Dems had a big group of 16 members. So, everybody was new, we had a few teething problems as a result.

Former MPs and the Scottish Parliament

While most of the staff and MSPs involved in the early days of the Parliament were entering politics at this level for the first time, around one tenth of the members elected in 1999 had served as Members of Parliament in London at some point in their careers. Taking up many of the most senior positions in their respective parties, they held a powerful influence in the new Parliament. They brought with them a wealth of parliamentary experience, and a clearer idea of doing things than many of their greener colleagues. In line with an informal cross-party agreement, the MPs who won seats in the Scottish Parliament did not immediately resign their positions, but instead waited until the next UK general election in 2001 to stand down their seats. This left a number of politicians in the testing scenario of serving as members in two parliaments, 400 miles apart, at the same time.

Making the move from Westminster was not an easy decision, even for the most committed supporters of devolution. Indeed, the great majority of Scottish MPs chose to remain in the House of Commons. Henry McLeish and Dennis Canavan take the chance to describe their own reasons for trading London for Edinburgh. The first Presiding Officer, and most experienced politician to come to the new Parliament, David Steel then remarks on the influence of the block of former MPs on the Parliament. The SNP's John Swinney discusses the difficulties he and his colleagues faced as they attempted to balance their dual roles as both MPs and MSPs in the years between 1999 and 2001. Finally, Bill Thomson, at the time a senior member of SPCB staff, makes the point that Westminster experience did not necessarily translate into expertise in the Scottish Parliament, causing a degree of discomfort for some.

HENRY MCLEISH, Former Labour Party MSP, Scottish Labour Leader and First Minister

At that time, Westminster was a big, significant and important place on the world stage. It was like the Kremlin, or the United States Congress, it was a big player. I had been there for more than a decade, so I had got used to that atmosphere, I was used to the big issues. The Scottish Parliament was a national Parliament on a smaller scale. I would be coming back to something that was a bit more modest, something very different to Westminster. We would have to build our history, we didn't have anything to look back on apart from the pre-1707 Parliament. So, there were big things going through my head. When I was deciding whether to move up to the Scottish Parliament, a number of issues made up my mind. Firstly, I had been instrumental in taking the devolution legislation through. I felt a sort of moral obligation to see it through. Very few MPs came back to Scotland. But I felt I had been a part of the team, I had advocated that this was going to be a powerful Parliament that would be good for Scots, it would not be sensible politics for me to turn my back on it and say, 'That's fine, but I'm going to stay at Westminster'. More positively, here was an opportunity to put an imprint on the new Parliament and take on a new challenge. I had no idea how this Parliament was going to develop, but I thought it would be something interesting to be a part of. Finally, it would be in Edinburgh. When you are an MP you go to London on a Monday. You have long nights, Tuesday, Wednesday, Thursday. You go back on a Thursday night or a Friday. But here was a situation where Scots could be involved in their Parliament, be involved in their constituencies, and have more time with their community and family.

DENNIS CANAVAN, Former Independent MSP

I foresaw that most of the bread and butter issues that would affect my constituents the most, things like health, education, housing, the environment, were going to be dealt with by the Scottish Parliament. These are the things that most constituency casework deals with. That was my main reason for wanting to go over to the Scottish Parliament. I also foresaw that more powers would likely be devolved to the Scottish Parliament in the fullness of time, and even the possibility of a Scottish Parliament becoming independent. So, I saw the power of Westminster on the decrease, whereas those of the Scottish Parliament would gradually increase.

DAVID STEEL, Former Presiding Officer and Liberal Democrat MSP

At the beginning it was important for the Parliament to have some MSPs with Westminster experience present. I think we could have done with more former MPs making the switch. I think that more would have come up if they had realised just how effective the Scottish Parliament was going to be. I have spoken to some of them about that, it's not just a theory. A lot of people felt regretful that they hadn't made the move. But once it was up and running, when we were through the first four years, I don't think it would have been a good thing having more retreads from the House of Commons coming up. By then, it was better to have new people coming in. But at the start, we could have done with a few more members with political experience to help us establish ourselves.

JOHN SWINNEY, Scottish National Party MSP, Deputy First Minister and Former Scottish National Party Leader

Being an MSP and MP at the same time was horrendous. Sometimes you had to literally be in two places at the same time. It was politically embarrassing at times, because you might miss important votes in one Parliament or the other, or otherwise not be where you were needed. You can't be in two places at once. There were politicians from all parties in the same situation, Jim Wallace, Sam Galbraith, there were a number of us. So, nobody was really turning it into a political issue. But I wouldn't advise it. It put you under real personal physical strain. I used to leave the Scottish Parliament, fly to London to vote, get the sleeper train back to Scotland, do my business here and then get on another plane to London.

It was no good for your health. I would not recommend it. It was politically embarrassing and personally unsustainable.

BILL THOMSON, Former SPCB Assistant Chief Executive

Amongst the members who were first elected in 1999, there was a reasonable number who had been involved in parliamentary work at Westminster. But the procedures of the Scottish Parliament were different. So, even these more experienced members weren't familiar with them. It took time for them to become comfortable with the way things had been set up here, and the way our practises were developing. Gradually, their confidence grew and their ability to use our procedures to their advantage politically developed. I didn't perceive a culture clash between the former mps and the way we were doing things up here. I did have, sometimes heated, discussions behind the scenes with people from all different parties who were involved in organising parliamentary business. Occasionally we were asked, 'That's what happens at Westminster, why aren't we doing it here?' But I don't think there was a general wish to replicate Westminster here in the Scottish Parliament, even among the former mps, I think there was generally more pride in doing things our own way.

The New Politics

A New Electoral System

Prior to the advent of devolution, elections at all levels of government in mainland Britain had used the first-past-the-post electoral system for generations. This system was criticised by the creators of the Scottish Parliament for producing non-proportional outcomes. In the 1997 general election, the Labour Party won more than three quarters of Scottish seats with less than half the vote. With a little over a fifth of the vote the SNP won six seats, and with a little less than a fifth the Conservatives didn't win anyway. Meanwhile, the Liberal Democrats secured ten seats with just 13 per cent of the vote. Minor parties had almost no chance of gaining parliamentary representation.

Instead, the Parliament adopted the additional member system. Voters were given two votes to cast. One was used to elect one of 73 constituency MSPs through traditional first-past-the-post contests. The other elected 56 members from the regional list through a system of proportional representation. As a result, the number of seats that each party won was much closer to its level of popular support. Despite being the most popular party, Labour fell short of winning a majority. The SNP won in only a handful of constituencies, yet secured its position as the main opposition by electing a large number of regional MSPs. The Conservatives elected all their members through the list. Notably, the Greens and Scottish Socialists each won one seat each to become parliamentary parties for the first time in their history.

Murdo Fraser comments on the way in which this new voting system shaped the Scottish Parliament, while Tommy Sheridan observes the tremendous impact the opportunity to elect an MSP had on the SSP.

MURDO FRASER, Conservative & Unionist Party MSP

The electoral system has allowed for a much more representative Parliament than would have been possible if we had used the standard Westminster first-past-the-post system. In the very first Parliament, the majority of constituency seats were held by Labour and the Lib Dems, and both the SNP and Conservatives were heavily biased towards the list. The Conservatives had no seats at all at Westminster, but we had 18 seats in the Scottish Parliament. We also had the voice of the smaller parties such as the Greens and Scottish Socialists, which would not have been possible under some other voting system. That offered us a Parliament that was much more representative of the country. On the whole, I think this has had a positive influence. Different voices have been represented, and it has been much harder for any one party to dominate the Scottish Parliament than is the case in Westminster. The SNP got an overall majority in 2011, but that was very unusual. In general, there have been more opportunities for opposition parties to have influence on the government.

TOMMY SHERIDAN, Former Scottish Socialist Party and Solidarity Convener and MSP

Electing an MSP in 1999 was absolutely critical for the SSP. Whether we like it or not, the question of credibility depends on being taken seriously. If you are with a party that has no representation at a local and, more importantly, parliamentary level, it is very difficult to be taken seriously.

You can't command media coverage, you can't make it onto political programmes and you don't have a platform. A platform is vital if you want to communicate ideas and policies. If the SSP hadn't broken through in 1999, then we would have remained a fringe group for years to come. I was on the Glasgow City Council, so we would have had a councillor, but that's nothing compared to having the voice to speak to the whole of Scotland on Scottish-wide issues.

Being in the Parliament was like a crusade for me. I used the position to effectively go on a tour of Scotland. I engaged with thousands of people in small meetings of a hundred here and a hundred there in every part of the country. We built up a socialist movement. None of that existed beforehand. Why would it exist? Before 1999 people asked, 'Who are the SSP? Why join the SSP? What can they do for you?' But once I was elected, I could fight for the issues I believed in. I wasn't just some dafty standing with a megaphone on a street corner, this was somebody who was actually in the Parliament. I used the parliamentary process to promote issues of importance. I was leading high profile parliamentary campaigns around the Warrant Sales Bill and free school meals. I was getting involved in a lot of political programmes like *Question Time*. My ideas were becoming credible with the public.

The Three Amigos – Canavan, Harper and Sheridan

All but three of the 129 MSPs elected in 1999 were drawn from the country's large established parties – Labour, the Scottish National Party, the Conservatives and the Liberal Democrats. The only exceptions were the Independent MSP Dennis Canavan, Robin Harper of the Greens and the Scottish Socialist Party's Tommy Sheridan. Each was an enigmatic figure in their own right. Dennis Canavan had served as the Labour MP for West Stirlingshire, later Falkirk West, since 1974. As a long-term advocate of devolution, he had been eager to make the move to the new Scottish Parliament, but fell afoul of his party leadership and was denied the chance to stand as a Labour candidate, despite the protests of his local party. In response, he put himself forward as an Independent and won the largest majority in the country at the first Scottish Parliamentary elections. Robin Harper had been a leading figure in Scottish and British Green politics since the party had been a tiny organisation with a handful of members and a nonexistent public profile. Erudite and well-mannered, he campaigned relentlessly for the party for years until finally winning his seat in the Scottish Parliament, becoming the first Green parliamentarian to be elected anywhere in the United Kingdom. With a background in the far left Militant Tendency, Tommy Sheridan came to prominence in the late 1980s and early 1990s through prominent campaigns against the poll tax and warrant sales that led to him being given a jail sentence in 1992. Having secured a local following, he won election to Glasgow Council in 1992. He then played a key role in bringing a number of radical socialist groups together to form the SSP ahead of the opening of the Scottish Parliament, creating a platform on which he was propelled into parliamentary office. The three went on to become some of the most recognisable members of the Parliament's first cohort. Sometimes collaborating, but usually operating individually, they challenged the major parties, spearheaded political campaigns and made an impression in the chamber.

Each of the three recall their efforts to make their voices heard and promote the issues that were important to them during the Parliament's first session.

DENNIS CANAVAN, Former Independent MSP

I adjusted to being an Independent politician fairly easily. I had always been regarded as a 'man o independent mind'. I didn't rely on speeches written by party researchers. I certainly never believed that the party whips should tell me what to say and how to vote. So, I adjusted fairly well. In the Scottish Parliament, I only had two members of staff – a constituency secretary and a research assistant. I found it liberating being outside of party politics. I no longer had party whips and party bosses breathing down my neck and telling me how to vote. I had always found the control freakery of the party bosses to be frustrating. When I looked around the Scottish Parliament I could see even more control freakery than at Westminster, because the party groups are smaller and more easily controlled. It certainly seemed to me that the party bosses were telling MSPs how to vote on virtually every occasion. That was worse than at Westminster.

I was blessed with a loud voice, so I was able to make my presence felt in the Scottish Parliament. With my past parliamentary experience from the House of Commons, I knew how to use opportunities, how to exploit opportunities and even create opportunities to get my tuppence worth in. For example, in the very early days of the Parliament I stood for First

Minister. I knew I had no chance of being elected as First Minister, but it gave me the opportunity to take part in one of the first debates ever to take place in the Parliament, and to put forth my alternate programme. I was to speak out on issues that I felt very strongly about. I also knew how to use question time, again from my experience of Westminster. I was once in the *Guinness Book of Records* for having asked more oral parliamentary questions than anyone else, so I had that experience of putting down questions and putting ministers on the spot to make the government more accountable to the Parliament and the people. I looked at the Standing Orders, and knew how to use them to get my point across – sometimes using a Point of Order, real or bogus, to get my point across. I also knew how to initiate members' debates, despite the fact that speaking time in these debates were, and I think still are, allocated according to the proportional support of each political party. These aren't supposed to be party debates. In the Scottish Parliament it was the party bosses who decided. So, I had to suck up to the party bosses, because I otherwise had no right to speak in members' debates. I used persuasion, and I was able to get a few things through, particularly for the people who I represented in Falkirk West.

I think the Parliament could have done more to accommodate members who were outside the party system. It was difficult for me at first, because I was the only Independent MSP elected in 1999. There were others from small parties – Robin Harper of the Greens and Tommy Sheridan from the Scottish Socialist Party. But I was the only Independent. I think the three of us were deemed not to be a big enough group, even if we did join up together, to get on the Scottish Parliamentary Bureau, a body that has huge influence in shaping the agenda of the Parliament. The three of us never formed a formal group, but we sometimes had discussions on certain issues and tried to come together on decisions that we agreed on. We also came to a decision on which committees we should be on. We were again at the tail of the queue, because committee places were also awarded according to the strength of the parties.

ROBIN HARPER, Former Scottish Green Party MSP and Co-convener

I had a whole lot of ways of making my influence felt. I got onto the Transport and Environment Committee, and I'm proud to say that I had a considerable influence on the National Parks Bill. I got a commitment from the then minister Sarah Boyack that the Bill would maintain the principle that if there is a conflict between economic progress and the environment, then the environment should always come first. That was within the spirit of the Bill. I also made sure to attend the chamber as much as possible. I think that the record books show that I attended more debates in the chamber than any other MSP. I kept a track of what Tommy Sheridan got up to, and I beat him, I spoke in more debates than he did. I just kept making interventions to put Green points of view forward in as many debates as I could. Another way I tried to push Green ideas in the debating chamber was to show that I could listen to other members. I would name check anybody who I though made a good point, refer to their statements in my speeches and make myself open to interventions. I would leave a minute's space in all my speeches for interventions. I think that helped me build up a reputation as a professional MSP who was there to listen as well as make my own points.

Looking back, I feel now is the time to review and improve all of the Parliament's procedures. No committees should be chaired by government party MSPs. We should have a Public Accounts Committee that roasts ministers Westminster-style, and the whole emphasis should move from First Minister's Questions, which is a joke, to professional and in depth questioning by committees. The fourth way I went about taking these things forward was to work very closely with cross-party groups that were close to core Green thinking. I was involved in lots of different types of groups. I wanted to show that the Greens weren't a one-trick pony, but had thoughts and policies across the policy spectrum. We could have been put into the open-toed sandals hippy box. We could have been sidelined. We wanted to look and sound professional. But I didn't abandon my signature rainbow-coloured scarf, because it was a very useful totem! I think the public liked it so I carried on wearing it.

TOMMY SHERIDAN, Former Scottish Socialist Party and Solidarity Convener and MSP

After I was elected, I looked at the rules of the Parliament, I looked at the Private Members' Bill process. But I had never written a Bill, and I didn't know how to write one. I found out that it was a very specialised skill. So, I went to the parliamentary research offices and said, 'Look, I need help with this Bill', and none of them could help me. There was no help for MSPs. I had to go outside of the Parliament to Mike Daly at the Govan Law Centre, who was very supportive of the Abolition of Warrant Sales Bill I wanted to introduce. He had never written a Bill before either, but he went away to study the rules and wrote an absolutely brilliant Bill. So brilliant in fact, that it became the first Private Members' Bill to pass. For all the fantastic research work the Parliament offered to support my Bill proposals, the weakness was that they didn't have a legal office to support you with Bills.

Coalition Government

While the new electoral system gave a wider parliamentary platform for minority voices, it also made it far more difficult for a single party to win an absolute majority of seats in the chamber. Indeed, this had been a deliberate objective of the schemes outlined in the Constitutional Convention, which imagined that no one party would ever be able to dominate in the Scottish Parliament. Just as was envisioned, there was no majority in 1999 as Labour fell nine seats short despite finishing well ahead of its nearest rival. As a result, it negotiated a coalition with the Liberal Democrats to run the Scottish Executive, the Parliament's government, together. Many in both parties, the press and the country at large were uneasy with this situation. Britain had not seen a multi-party government since the Second World War, meaning that most were unfamiliar with the workings of coalition politics. Nonetheless, the coalition held together for eight years, dominating the first decade of the Parliament's history.

The Liberal Democrat leader Jim Wallace describes the difficult negotiations that led to the first coalition agreement in 1999. Two members of the Scottish Executive during the coalition, the former First Minister Jack McConnell and one-time minister Jackie Baillie of the Labour Party, the rebellious Liberal Democrat backbencher Mike Rumbles, and Andrew Nicoll of the *Scottish Sun* newspaper then discuss the, at times fractious, relationship between the two parties of government that ensued in the years that followed.

JIM WALLACE, Former Liberal Democrat MSP, Scottish Liberal Democrat Leader and Deputy First Minister

We in the Liberal Democrats always knew it would be a possibility that we might enter government. After all, we had been the ones who had been the prime movers in ensuring that we got a system of proportional representation for the Scottish Parliament. Which in all likelihood was going to lead to a situation in which we had no overall majority. Therefore, we had mentally attuned ourselves to the possibility. The reality was something different. It was never going to be at any price, everything hinged on getting an agreement that would be a basis for government. In marked contrast to the Labour Party, we had given this some thought. The Labour Party thought they would just incorporate us into a continuing Labour government. That was their attitude. They were the sitting government in Westminster, they controlled the Scottish Office, we would add our numbers to them and the ship would just continue to sail as it had before. There was a Liberal Democrat stalwart called Philip Goldenberg who had created a draft on how we might have gone about coalition talks had the 1992 general election produced no overall majority, he sent that to me to look at for advice. So, we had prepared ourselves well in advance.

When I first met Donald Dewar, I told him I wanted a programme for government, and he said, 'What's that?' I told him that we wanted to set out what we would do in government. He produced three or four handwritten pages, and I produced around 28. I felt the final version was much closer to ours than Labour's. It was not going to be easy. They were pretty fraught talks, they almost broke down on a couple of occasions. I had to prepare myself mentally for the possibility that we would walk away with no agreement. There were at least two occasions that I thought it wasn't going to work. There were pizzas after midnight and endless talks, I was absolutely shattered.

One of the problems was that when we actually reached an agreement with Labour, our party couldn't recognise why we hadn't managed to get our whole manifesto through. They didn't seem to realise that we were the smaller party by some margin! In the end, I had three of my MSPs vote against the agreement when we put it to the vote, while 13 supported me. Part of the problem we were facing was the culture. In a UK general election, a van comes up outside Downing Street in the morning and it's changed. I never expected an agreement within 24 hours, I had the idea it might take a bit longer. But the media was saying, 'Scotland is ungoverned!' The Parliament wasn't even taking the powers until July. It was all nonsense. But it was the culture that we had.

In 1999, the civil service was deferential to the Labour Party. Donald

Dewar may have been the leader of the largest party in the Scottish Parliament, but he was also the Secretary of State for Scotland. I don't think the civil servants could get their head around the fact that there was a difference between being Secretary of State for Scotland and leader of the largest party, and already being First Minister of Scotland. We found that any briefings that we were getting had already been cleared by Labour ministers and SPADs before they got to us. That was very irritating at the time, but it was a product of the system. By 2003, I was Deputy First Minister, and therefore the civil service was as anxious to support me as they were to support the First Minister during the coalition negotiations. So, we were on far more equal terms in 2003 than we had been in 1999. In the 2003 negotiations, we were better prepared, the Labour Party was better prepared and the civil service was better prepared.

JACK MCCONNELL, Former Labour Party MSP, Scottish Labour Leader and First Minister

I was quite relaxed about the coalition, partly because it was a reality and partly because I had worked within the Constitutional Convention alongside the Liberal Democrats and smaller parties in the 1990s. I was used to working on a consensus basis. I felt it was probably quite a good thing in the early years not to have one party in total control. I think many of the parliamentarians found it more difficult. Some came from a local government background. They were used to decisions being made within party groups and then driven through without a great deal of debate. Some MSPs came from Westminster, where they were also used to majority government. Some people found it difficult to work in a coalition where they had to explain their decisions and persuade their colleagues more than they were used to. But I relished it. I always felt that because we weren't acting in as tribal a way as political parties normally do, we were making better decisions.

When I took over as First Minister in 2001, it was towards the end of that four-year Parliament. We already had a coalition agreement with the Liberal Democrats. I regarded it as a commitment between the two parties, but also to Donald Dewar, that we should try to see through the initial agreement made in 1999 as much as possible. I was able to inject some of my own personal priorities and ideas into the final 18 months of that Parliament. But most of the work was around pursuing, or in some cases rescuing, some of the commitments that had been made earlier. Things changed in 2003 after I had the opportunity as First Minister to set a manifesto, win an election campaign, and really properly get to work in a tone that was shaped by my personal approach to politics.

The dynamic within the coalition was affected by the change in the numbers in 2003. After the election, the balance between Labour and the Liberal Democrats was slightly more in the direction of the Liberal Democrats. The type of coalition was different as well. In 1999, the coalition had basically been a few Liberal Democrat ideas added into the Labour manifesto, with one or two things taken out. In 2003, we had gone into the election with fresh manifestos, designed in Scotland, made for Scotland. The 2003 coalition agreement was very much a negotiated settlement between those two manifestos. It was more in the European style, a much better way of making decisions. But it was based on the experience we had had in the previous four years. So, it was different. We also had better relationships for the resolution of disputes, for early warning on problems, for discussions. That had been a problem in the first four years. It was very good that we did that. I think it is recognised that those four years were among the most productive of the Scottish Parliament in terms of legislation and big initiatives. Through those four years, our government had a majority of four seats in the Parliament! If anybody decided to vote the other way, either from the Labour or the Liberal Democrat side, our legislation wouldn't pass. I think we only lost one vote in the Parliament chamber in those four years. For a coalition in testing circumstances, with a lot of quite strong individuals in both the ministerial team and the backbenches, that was a quite a remarkable achievement. We addressed that tighter arithmetic by having a more settled coalition with a properly negotiated settlement. The ministerial team was also more experienced, we were more prepared, we were hungrier for change, we had a set programme for change. We worked hard with both the coalition parties to maintain the right level of support. Ministers worked really hard to win the public arguments and to prepare good quality legislation. The two parties worked together better in that second session that they had in the first.

JACKIE BAILLIE, Labour Party MSP

The Lib Dems were hugely difficult to work with. Not the ministers, you had really decent people in the ministerial team that I got on with, it was their backbenches that were just off the wall. So, the hard negotiations weren't so much at administrative levels, it was backbench to backbench. It was a creative challenge, and very interesting. Certainly, in the area I was in, community and social justice, they didn't have a strong interest. So, I would find myself negotiating from time to time, but not often. They did bring stability to government by and large, working across the cabinet was not an issue with them, it was just the backbenches. They had some interesting people, like Donald Gorrie, but he was one of life's awkward people. People like him were insistent on getting their way. Generally, people came to accommodations with each other. But around election time it could get difficult. Prior to elections, we both wanted to distinguish ourselves from each other, so it made things slightly sensitive. So, it depended on the issue and electoral cycle, and you always had awkward people in both groups. They could be awkward at any time, but on the whole it was a good relationship.

MIKE RUMBLES, Liberal Democrat MSP

I had mixed feelings about going into coalition with the Labour Party. When I had been in the army I hadn't been allowed to speak my mind about politics. When I came out I wanted to talk about my Liberalism, and going into coalition would put another constraint on what we could say publicly. I did think it was important that we were in government and were able to change things for the better, but I wasn't very keen on being too close to the Labour Party. Right at the beginning it was proposed that we should have joint parliamentary party meetings between Labour and the Liberal Democrats – which I absolutely balked at. If I had wanted to join the Labour Party I would have joined the Labour Party. I didn't, I'm a Liberal. That is one of the reasons why I voted against the coalition government 41 times in the chamber. I felt that either we had not been strong enough in our negotiations with the Labour Party, or the government was proposing things that I saw as illiberal and I wouldn't have it.

Throughout the life of the government, the ministers got on far better together than the backbenches did. The backbenches were almost excluded. I remember group meetings where our leader Jim Wallace would come into the room and tell us what the government was going to do rather than saying that this was one position and this was another. Things were already decided before we heard about them. Both he and the ministers tended to defend the decisions they had already made with their Labour colleagues, rather than explain where we were coming from. That led to a lot of tensions within the group. I still think to this day that the ministers didn't understand why we were unhappy with this and people like me would vote against them. It was a sharp contrast to how the Liberals operated in coalition in the House of Commons between 2010 and 2015, when, in my view, there weren't enough rebellions from the backbenches. We were better able to keep our identity, and did rather better in the 2003 elections and even the 2007 election than our colleagues in Westminster did after being in coalition government.

ANDREW NICOLL, Associate Editor of the *Scottish Sun*

It was a bit disappointing. We were told that the proportional electoral system would create rainbow alliances, and that people would bleed in and out from either side of the party groups. The Parliament would be a coming together of minds. But that didn't happen. Westminster thinking pervaded on all sides for a long time. Donald Dewar took the view that you had to have a majority in order to govern. So, he joined up with the Lib Dems and created this unmovable block. It was set on the same ridged tramlines that they have at Westminster.

I remember when the coalition was first secured, we in the media were invited to the National Museum to see Donald Dewar and Jim Wallace sign their agreement. We were being held behind a velvet rope, and I asked a Labour staffer why we were here, and he replied, 'Because the railway carriage at Compiègne was not available'. Quite clearly, the Labour Party regarded this as an abject surrender by the Lib Dems. It wasn't a partnership in any real sense. The Lib Dems were very much the junior partners. That became clear as time went by, and became particularly clear during the second Executive. Whenever there was good news a Labour minister would announce it, if there was ever bad news then a Lib Dem was pushed out. They were the bad news guys.

Challenging Days

The Death of Donald Dewar

Donald Dewar possessed huge political authority that was critical to the Scottish Parliament in its first months. He had decades of parliamentary experience, was a veteran of the Home Rule movement, and held genuine stature on the UK-stage as the only MSP to have ever served in the British Cabinet. His key role in bringing the Parliament into being as the last Secretary of State for the old Scottish Office and the first First Minister of the new Scottish Executive, had led to some honouring him as the 'Father of the Nation'. Today, a 9-foot statue of him stands on Glasgow's Buchanan Street, overlooking the city he represented for over 20 years. Within Holyrood itself, the Donald Dewar Library stands in memory to his contribution to the Parliament's birth. His health had begun to worsen around one year into his tenure as First Minister. In April 2000 he was admitted to hospital, undergoing surgery in May. He initially appeared to have recovered, returning to work in August, before leaving the nation in shock as he passed away on 11 October following a brain haemorrhage.

Four of his colleagues, two of the senior members of Dewar's cabinet and the men who succeeded him as First Minister, Henry McLeish and Jack McConnell, alongside the Labour backbencher Johann Lamont, and the Deputy First Minister Jim Wallace describe their personal grief, the impact of his loss on the institution and the ways in which the Parliament attempted to move forward from this tragic blow to the devolution project.

JOHANN LAMONT, Labour Party MSP and Former Scottish Labour Leader

It would have been on either a radio or television bulletin that I heard them say that he had fallen. I had a call from John Reid which wasn't reassuring. It was very neutral, and you thought something terrible must have happened, it was really shocking. Then the next day, we were brought into a room in the old Lothian Regional building as a Labour group and were told that he had passed away. I remember Tom McCabe, our business manager, being utterly stunned. The room was really quiet. People didn't really know what to say, but we were gathering support for each other. Karen Gillon, one of the young women MSPs elected in that first Parliament, she had just had her first child and was feeling so emotional about everything. It stuck in my mind, that feeling of being bereft, because he was so much at the centre of giving us confidence in what we were trying to do as we were trying to learn the job. All of a sudden, we thought, 'What do we do now?'

HENRY MCLEISH, Former Labour Party MSP, Scottish Labour Leader and First Minister

Donald's death had a devastating impact on the Parliament. That doesn't need to be measured in material terms. He understood devolution. He saw it as a journey, not a destination. Once the genie was out of the bottle there was no going back, he wasn't sure where things would lead but knew Scotland was going on a great new path. Very few people, especially in the Labour Party, understood these ideas at the time, but they were a powerful sentiment. He had been the key individual in the project. Since 1997, Donald had been the go-to man for devolution. He had great stature, he was a great thinker, he was very erudite, he had great delivery. His death was a huge loss to a project that was barely under way. We were still bedding in, still finding our feet. Then, that key piece of continuity disappeared.

JIM WALLACE, Former Liberal Democrat MSP, Scottish Liberal Democrat Leader and Deputy First Minister

There were huge pressures when I took on the role of Acting First Minister. It had been a part of our partnership agreement for the coalition, but it was a scenario no one had really foreseen. I remember he told me he was going to hospital for tests, but it was more than likely he would need to have surgery, and he told me that I would have to go on and take over. He said, 'Deputies, deputise'. And that was it. Oddly enough, Donald's illness helped to cement the coalition. People had these daft notions that since I had become Acting First Minister I would start enacting all sorts of whacky Liberal Democrat policies. But we had a partnership agreement, it was never anticipated that this aspect of the partnership agreement would be used, but the situation solidified it. But we were all shattered when Donald passed away.

JACK MCCONNELL, Former Labour Party MSP, Scottish Labour Leader and First Minister

It was an exceptionally sad moment when Donald Dewar passed away. That affected everybody, friend and foe. It also created a faster move on to the stage beyond Donald. He had been the obvious person to be the first First Minister, he was the established figurehead of the institution. Alongside the Presiding Officer David Steel, he represented the history of campaigns for a Scottish Parliament. His death meant that the Parliament had to move on to a new chapter very quickly, where we had to focus on the present rather than our history. The circumstances were awful, but it did give all of us a wakeup call that we had to rise to the occasion, stop relying on the older figures and take our own decisions on where we wanted to take the Parliament.

Media Relations

In its first years, the Scottish Parliament endured an incredibly difficult relationship with the media. Even beyond the ever present and looming issue of the Holyrood building project, it was confronted with a seemingly relentless stream of bad news stories and criticisms. The policies the Executive put forward were derided as either uninspired or unwanted, colouring public opinion of devolution more generally despite the separation of the Executive and Parliament, while the standard of its MSPs was labelled as sub-par and the Parliament faced a series of damaging scandals and resignations. Some depicted it as a 'toytown Parliament', unfit for purpose and deserving of abolition. This relationship developed in a substantially different media context than exists in Scotland today. Newspapers in particular were vastly more influential, with readerships several times greater than they are now, and had correspondingly greater resources. This wider reach ensured that the press had the power to cause serious concern for the Parliament, and they did so on a seemingly daily basis.

Colin Mackay describes the emergence of the large and powerful parliamentary press pack that so discomforted the Parliament in its early days. The then Presiding Officer David Steel then notes his surprise and disappointment in the way in which this relationship developed.

COLIN MACKAY, Holyrood Editor for *STV News*

There was a lot of excitement about the start of the Scottish Parliament journalistically, because it was a big new institution that meant that Scottish politics could be reported on a daily basis for the first time. Before that, Westminster by-elections had been really exciting for Scottish journalists because there was a Scottish political news story on their patch every day for a little while. But with the start of the Scottish Parliament, there was potentially Scottish political news on your doorstep every day of the week. So, every journalist organisation, every news outlet, was looking at expanding its political coverage in Scotland. What was at that time Scottish Radio Holdings, now Bauer, a large group of Scottish radio stations, had never had anyone covering politics. But given the Parliament was opening, they decided they should recruit somebody, and that was how I started working at the Parliament. It was across the industry. Radio Scotland had a nightly programme from the Scottish Parliament on the days it was sitting. It doesn't do that now. If you looked at the newspapers, you had seven people from the *Daily Record* in the Parliament, they are down to two now. You had four or five at *The Herald*, they're down to two now. The *Scotsman* had a big team, everybody had big teams covering the Scottish Parliament. It was new and it was exciting and every single thing you did was a new story. That had an effect. The more journalists you have, the more people looking for a story, the more people looking for an exclusive story, the more scrutiny you are going to get. There was a lot of scrutiny of the Parliament in those days.

DAVID STEEL, Former Presiding Officer and Liberal Democrat MSP

My aim as the first Presiding Officer was to make sure that the Parliament established a good reputation. It was quite fragile early on. We had a mixed press. It was a bit hard, for example, when we got flak for the decision taken at Westminster to give every new MSP in 1999 a bronze medallion as a souvenir. One of the papers had a headline complaining that the first thing the new MSPs had done was award themselves medals. That decision had nothing to do with the Scottish Parliament! That sort of thing was very annoying, and I was quite cross about it at the time. We had a tricky relationship with the media. I had a go at them at the press awards in Glasgow for their journalism. I had, perhaps naïvely, thought that the press would be more supportive of what the Parliament was doing. It only gradually dawned on me that it wasn't going to be easy. But, for all that, the relationship did improve over time.

The Resignation of Henry McLeish

Donald Dewar's successor, Henry McLeish, held the office of First Minister for just one year. He was driven to resign in November 2001 by the 'Officegate' issue. This referred to a controversy relating to the sub-letting of space in his constituency office to a law firm during his time as MP for Central Fife. This technical question of parliamentary standards quickly escalated into a serious political issue. The police announced that they were investigating a complaint relating to McLeish's offices, he was fiercely criticised in the media and even the parliamentary chamber, and struggled to justify himself in public. His well-remembered explanation that the affair represented, 'A muddle, not a fiddle', failed to win confidence in his leadership. Faced with this pressure, Henry McLeish resigned as First Minister. He was soon replaced by the Parliament's third First Minister in just two years as Jack McConnell took on the role that he would occupy until 2007.

The Scottish Sun's Andrew Nicoll discusses the scandal from a media perspective, while Henry McLeish takes the chance to reflect on his resignation. Jack McConnell then describes the wider context of crisis the Parliament found itself in when he succeeded McLeish as First Minister.

ANDREW NICOLL, Associate Editor of *The Scottish Sun*

Henry McLeish had an unhappy time as First Minister. He lost his job over the 'Officegate' scandal regarding his office expenses. I don't believe for a second that Henry McLeish benefited from that arrangement. Nowadays, I don't think that sort of scandal would topple any politician, never mind a First Minister. The press had a bigger influence at that time. It was an issue that could roll on and on and on. Every time that Henry McLeish's press people managed to put a lid on the scandal, it would pop up some place else. It was just the same story repeated endlessly. I admit that we in the press were consciously trying to keep the issue going in the papers all the way to the weekend, when the Sunday papers would kick it up and we would have something else to go on. It became a war of attrition against poor Henry. One of his press officers came out with an idea that they would make all the information about the issue public and use the line, 'It's a muddle, not a fiddle' to explain the situation. Then the late great journalist Angus MacLeod responded by saying, 'So, you're not bent, you're just incompetent then?' It was over for him then.

HENRY MCLEISH, Former Labour Party MSP, Scottish Labour Leader and First Minister

A lot of people have said to me that a lot worse has happened to a lot of people since I stepped down. I was of course upset to step down, but I think it was the right thing to do. Once the press have the bit between their teeth, they are not going to go away. I had made mistakes, nothing more. I was paying a high price. My main concern at that point was that if I had carried on, I would take the spotlight away from the early days of the Parliament, where real progress was being made. By removing myself from the scene, you remove the problem overnight. I was disappointed, I felt I had let people down, but I felt it was the right thing to do. It is difficult to adjust after you have been prominent in politics and then go down to being a backbencher. The mood was soured and I was conscious that there were new people coming through. That was a difficult time. I had to move on, and once I left politics there has been a second coming for me.

JACK MCCONNELL, Former Labour Party MSP, Scottish Labour Leader and First Minister

When I look back to November 2001, we were in a real crisis. The building project was affecting everybody, we had had a series of scandals, sometimes around minor matters and sometimes more substantial ones, we had all the instability that comes with having three First Ministers in as many years, Alex Salmond, the leader of the main opposition party, had decided to return to Westminster, there had been resignations in other parties as well. There were people writing in late 2001 that the Scottish Parliament had been a mistake and we should go back to the old system. That was not an extreme position in late 2001. So, when I replaced Henry McLeish as First Minister, I knew that I had a very immediate objective to stabilise the ship and ensure that the Parliament became properly embedded in Scottish life. I thought once that was achieved we could have greater ambitions and look towards the future. But the immediate task was to steady things and rebuild public confidence in the parliamentarians and the institution itself.

The Holyrood Project

The Building Process

The Holyrood building was one of the most troubled construction projects of recent times to take place anywhere in Scotland, Britain and even
beyond. Woefully over budget and years behind schedule, it was the subject of an official inquiry before even opening its doors. Lord Fraser's
report criticised large parts of the process from start to finish. Certainly,
the Project had been deeply unfortunate to lose its two most passionate
advocates in the architect Enric Miralles and its political driving force,
the First Minister Donald Dewar, in the space of a few months in 2000.
Yet it clearly suffered from a degree of mismanagement throughout its
lifetime, that contributed to the painful and continuous escalation of
costs and delays over the years.

Four individuals involved, to varying degrees, in different aspects and
at different times, in the process that brought Holyrood from an idea to
a physical reality shed light on its difficult history. Henry McLeish notes
some of the political origins of later difficulties, as Donald Dewar's determination to rush forward with the construction, and the focus of the
team involved in enacting devolution in the hectic period between 1997
and 1999 on other aspects of the new Parliament, drove considerations
of cost to the back of people's minds. This in turn led to the adoption of
an unrealistically low cost estimate that proved to be an albatross around
Holyrood's neck for years. Former Holyrood Project Team member John
Paterson discusses his involvement in the building project from its earliest stage, up to the opening of the Parliament and the deaths of Dewar
and Miralles. Willie Heigh then focuses on the overrunning costs, and
some of the reasons for their escalation over the years. The Clerk and
Chief Executive Paul Grice admits to the personal strains the building
Project put on him in his leadership position.

HENRY MCLEISH, Former Labour Party MSP, Scottish Labour Leader and First Minister

I think the main problem was that when we got to Westminster and were
devising the Parliament, a new building was the least of our concerns.
In fact, it wasn't even a concern. When we were asked to put a price on

it, we gave them a quote of the cost that was incredibly out of place, because it bore no relation to anything. It was a figure plucked completely out of thin air, a convenience in the civil service. Of course, it didn't cost anything like that. But no one was focused on that. This was a new Parliament, new legislation, 129 new members – this was a big deal. And all of a sudden, we were being asked these sort of details. This is one of the reasons I suggested we leave it to later, and allow the MSPs to decide once the Parliament had opened. But Donald Dewar wanted to forge ahead. The cost was wildly out, it was unrealistic at the start. As the building started to grow arms and legs, the unrealistic first cost was held up as a source of criticism. We made our own difficulties out of that. We just didn't give the parliamentary building, or the cost of it, any significance because we had so many things to deal with at that point.

JOHN PATERSON, SPCB Security Programme Manager

I was one of four people in the project team that was scoping out what the needs of the new Parliament building would be. One of my very first duties was to go through the public engagement process regarding the four possible sites for the Parliament. That was St Andrew's House, Leith, Haymarket and Holyrood. So, I stood in the public chambers of the old Lothian council on George IV Bridge with display boards and engaged with the public and answered their questions. We quickly moved within a month to choosing Holyrood as the site, and then began the competition to find an architect. We put out the invitations to architects to do the design. Seventy architectural practices from around the world responded, we sifted that down to 12 and they were all asked to come up with a design interpretation. Of those, it was sifted down again to five or six, of which Miralles was one. They then all went through a competitive interview process. The Secretary of State, Donald Dewar, was the chair of the panel, and he was supported by the Scottish Office officials John Gibbons and Robert Gordon, and they were supported by two people from the world of architecture in Andy McMillan and Joanne O'Connor, and Kirsty Wark the BBC presenter was on that panel as well. They looked over the views of what the Parliament would look like. We had to be adaptable, all our interviews were in Edinburgh at Victoria Quay, but Donald Dewar got called to Westminster one day and we had to move the whole shooting match down to Westminster in London. That is where I first encountered Enric Miralles, little did I know at that time that he would be the successful candidate.

Everything moved very quickly. From the December of 1997, through to the end of 1998 we had appointed the architect and understood the design of the building. I had to deal with Scottish & Newcastle, who were the previous occupants of the Holyrood site. I had to manage their withdrawal from the site whilst allowing contractors and consultants access to the site, even though it didn't formally belong to us yet. We then had to deal with the demolition contractors, who were clearing the site. We also had a lot of archaeological work done, because of the historic value of the area, another challenging time. Henry McLeish came in to swing the wrecking ball for the first time, to symbolise the knocking down of the old building. I stayed on working at the site with the construction firm. It was amazing to see the building coming up from the ground. It was quite a challenging time when the Parliament opened up in May 1999. We now had elected members who felt they had played no part in the process. Some parties were especially opposed to the decisions Donald Dewar had made. Members were quite openly hostile to the building, to the location and to the process we had started. In the first couple of months it was really touch and go whether or not we were going to continue the project or if there would be a temporary stop. I think if the process had been stopped temporarily we would not be sitting in the building that we now have. It didn't get any easier from there. We suffered the loss of Donald Dewar and the loss of Enric Miralles in 2000. They had been the standard bearers of the project. When they were gone, it allowed people who had not been positive about the building to come forward and try to cause harm to the project. It was a great sense of pride and relief that it was all over when we finally managed to complete it.

WILLIE HEIGH, SPCB Head of Project and Programme Management

I have been at enough project management conferences where they always do a talk about projects that have gone wrong and they start with the Sydney Opera House and move on to Holyrood. Actually, these days they start on about the trams. My background is a surveyor and, it is interesting, one of the things they teach you early on when you are learning to be a surveyor is the first price you tell your client is the one they expect to pay at the end of the day. I think the Scotland Bill had something like an estimate of £10 million to £40 million for the building. I have no idea what that was based on, but it was clearly nonsense because I do not think we even had the remotest idea what the building would look like or what the size of it would be at that time.

It was really unfair to compare those kinds of figures and the timescales of when it might be done. I think they were basing that on some kind of bog standard office block down at Victoria Quay in Leith. You just needed to look at the place and realise that was never how it was going to be built at that cost. The vision was for an architecturally iconic place. If you look at the first couple of pages of the design brief, it lays out pretty clearly that it is a visionary place for Scotland. To compare it to £10 million to £40 million is crazy. By the time the design got done, I think it was up at the £195 million to £230 million point, even though it ended up costing £400 million.

I think there is multiple reasons it ended up costing so much in the end. The politics around it did not help. The complexity of the building did not help. It is very much a one-off. I do not think there is anything in here that you could point to and say that has been done before or that was easy. A lot of the stuff was ground breaking. It was extremely complex and very ambitious, so that did not help at all. I think there was a lot of ambition, probably stemming back from Donald Dewar, that architecturally it would be a statement and it would be iconic. But that did not match up with the statements of how quickly it would get built or what the cost would be.

PAUL GRICE, SPCB Clerk and Chief Executive

It was tough. I wasn't formally responsible for the building project until the summer of 1999, by which time it had been going for about a year and a half. Right from then until it was finished 5 years later it was really tough. There was intense pressure, media scrutiny, and we had a public inquiry before it was even finished. At one level that was not a sensible idea, but actually I thought that the great thing about it was that if we survived the inquiry then the pain would be out of the way by the time the building was open. We could then just get on with things. That is what happened in the end. I am quite a resilient person, but you don't find out how resilient you are until you are tested. I was reading my name in the headlines, walking among members, many of whom were opposed to Holyrood or very concerned about it, I was giving evidence frequently, I had to explain that the cost had gone up again and again, I was dealing with the builders and the architects. Some of that was grim.

Looking back, I could have done things better. I was slow to realise that it wasn't going well. My main focus had been on creating an effective Parliamentary Service. I don't think that it would have changed the course of history, it wouldn't have been built two years quicker for half the money, but if I had been a bit more ruthless and a bit more balanced in my attention that might have made a difference. If I had had the confidence to be much more up front with the politicians, to bring them together and say, 'We've got to stay in the room until we sort this out', that probably could have helped.

The Controversy and Its Effects

The troubles over the building project led to an eruption of media controversy. Negative stories and fierce critiques were relentless, and grew stronger as the issues with the construction piled up. Every aspect of the building caused ire. The fact that the key decisions had been made by the Scottish Office before the opening of the Parliament, the wider role of politicians in the process, the choice of location, the architect and his modernist designs, the construction company used and their practices, the lack of control the Parliament appeared to have over the project, and above all else, the escalating costs and delays, were all the subject of opposition. For the press, it was the story that never stopped giving, as it verged between the outrageous and the ridiculous on a monthly basis, while also being an area in which their serious scrutiny of the use of public money was clearly important. Through these years, the public mood darkened, turning sharply away from the Parliament as many voters became frustrated and even angry at the way the affair was being handled. The Parliament itself found it almost impossible to maintain any sort of control over public perceptions, or ease concerns. The institution as a whole, and many of the individuals who worked within it, were left deeply rattled by the ordeal.

Three individuals drawn from the media, members and SPCB staff offer differing perspectives on the controversy that unfolded. Journalist Colin Mackay describes the press perspective of the story. Linda Fabiani, a member of the team of MSPs overseeing the project and a keen advocate of Holyrood, discusses the opposition she encountered from both the media and her fellow MSPs. Shona Skakle meanwhile, describes the power of the controversy to spread angst far beyond those who were on the frontline, dealing with the construction or press relations, to the wider body of staff employed by the Parliament.

COLIN MACKAY, Holyrood Editor for *STV News*

I think there were times where the people in charge of the Parliament felt that they were in a bit of a bunker. Because the cost of the building had been set at 40 million, it was very hard to sell to the public that those costs would keep on rising. It went up to 100-odd million, then 200-odd, there were continual big rises. That was difficult to sell politically. It was massively late as well, and a lot of people at the time were uncomfortable about the design, which wasn't entirely practical. I think the Presiding Officer at the time, David Steel, found the criticism quite hard to take. He spoke about, 'Bitchy journalism' at one point, because there was a lot of sniping at the Parliament and parliamentary authorities. I think Donald Dewar found it quite difficult too. But there were times where it wasn't entirely transparent what was going on with the funding of the Parliament. There was a lot of criticism that was probably unfounded, but the scrutiny was never unfounded. That is partly what we in the media are for. It was the biggest building project in the country at the time, the highest profile, and I think the media was mostly justified in the way we dealt with it.

LINDA FABIANI, Scottish National Party MSP

I remember going to the very first presentation which Enric Miralles gave and instantly loved the project. I loved the building, I'd worked in construction for some time and I was never of the belief that it could be delivered for the costs put forward. I knew it was going to go way over budget and changes were made in order to make it run way overtime. None of that was a surprise to me at all. But I recognised how important it was. I felt the Parliament was ours after centuries and I wanted it to be special. So, when there were debates and politicking about it, I was frustrated. I felt there was a lot of dumbing down of the institution by the stances some people took. That was frustrating for me.

When there was a decision that each party should have a representative overseeing the construction project, I volunteered to be the member from the SNP. I suspect everyone thought it would be a career finisher, but it meant a lot to me, so I stuck with it right through to the bitter end.

It was a difficult time as even my own group was split as to whether we should take part or not. Split as to, how we should approach the whole subject of the Parliament building, whether we should be negative or positive about. There were views at the time that it should be abandoned and had become a bit of a white elephant. There was a huge amount of negativity from the press, as well as members of Parliament themselves. These things normally don't bother me, but there was one particular article in which a journalist said that the members of the progress group should be taken out and shot. That's the only bit of newspaper coverage that has ever got to me. The violent overtones within it and the nastiness in it. It was difficult as the pressure was constant, but I signed up for it so that's the way it was.

SHONA SKAKLE, SPCB Head of Enquiries

You couldn't fail to be affected by the building issue. Partly because we were all in interim accommodation waiting around to move, and the construction significantly overran. We were also in lots of different campuses around Edinburgh, so we didn't have the chance to get to know each other in the way you do when you are all in one central place. But there was also a period of time where that was all anybody spoke about. They weren't really looking at what the Parliament was actually trying to achieve, and what it was doing in relation to health and education and whatever else. They were just pointing to how much money it was costing, how far behind schedule it was and how it was wasting taxpayers' money. Every time you got into a taxi, if you said you worked in the Parliament that is all you would hear about. Quite often, if you were chatting to people outside of work about your job, that would be their reaction as well. Sometimes I would avoid saying where I worked. So, it did have an impact on us that way. It was something that obsessed people for quite a long time. It was hard when you were really enthusiastic about what you were doing, and trying to make a difference, but the building was all anybody wanted to talk about. I wouldn't say it dampened my enthusiasm for working at the Parliament, but it was disappointing. It felt like that was all the press and the public were focusing on.

PART 2

New Beginnings

2003–2011

Holyrood

The Move

THE SCOTTISH PARLIAMENT's relocation from its temporary accommodation in the General Assembly Rooms of the Church of Scotland, and a number of accompanying offices around the centre of Edinburgh, to the new Holyrood building in 2004 was a watershed moment in the institution's history.

Following the Parliament's second election in 2003, the new Presiding Officer George Reid brought a fresh impetus to completing the building project and moving in as soon as possible. Deadlines were set, arrangements made, and in the summer of 2004 Holyrood's new occupants began to arrive, with an official opening attended by the Queen taking place in October. At the time it was still at least partially a building site, with work ongoing while staff and MSPs sought to settle in – but the Parliament now had a home of its own for the first time. Although the Holyrood building's appearance divided the Scottish public, and continues to do so to this day, it was critically acclaimed – winning the Stirling Prize, Britain's most prestigious architectural award, in 2005. It also quickly developed into a major tourist attraction, with hundreds of thousands of visitors coming through its doors. More importantly, its opening provided release from the longest-running and most damaging saga in the Parliament's history, the building project itself. This was an opportunity to move past those problems, and look towards a brighter future, with a permanent home, improved facilities and fresh ambitions.

Yet, the move was not solely positive. For all its faults, the temporary accommodation had carried some charms that weren't replicated at Holyrood. Located much more in the heart of Edinburgh, and not shut off in a self-contained campus, some believed that the original site brought politics closer to the people and fostered a more relaxed environment as MSPs of all parties socialised, plotted, celebrated and commiserated with each other, journalists and even members of the public in the area's many watering holes. As the Scottish Parliament moved forward, this culture was left behind.

The role played by George Reid's force of personality in completing the move, and the sense of relief when it was over with, is depicted by Paul Grice. Bill Thomson, a key figure in planning the transition, discusses the challenges he faced in communicating with a construction team that had been jarred by years of criticism, and the tight timetable within which Holyrood could be opened. Willie Heigh notes the urgency of the last days of the build, and how close it came to not being ready, before discussing the almost farcical experience of handling the scramble of MSPs for the best available office spaces.

PAUL GRICE, SPCB Clerk and Chief Executive

A key moment was after the election in 2003. George Reid was exactly the right person to come in as Presiding Officer with a year to go and finish it. He had this utter conviction and he was fantastic to work with. We took a decision in January 2004, I remember us sitting and saying, 'If we book the Queen to open it, it has to be finished'. George understood that once we had invited Her Majesty and she had graciously accepted that was it. Once she's in the diary, she's in the diary. You don't ring up in September and say, 'Can we put you back three weeks Your Majesty?' So we had to move in on the August of that year, and we did.

After that, I went on holiday to Lanzarote with my family. The first couple of days, I was turbo-charged. I did a triathlon, went running, I was on cloud nine. Then on day three, I got ill and I was ill for the rest of the holiday. I was really poorly, couldn't leave my room. I think that the first two days were just adrenalin and then the stress and enormous pressure from those past five years kicked in. I wouldn't say it has been plain sailing since then, but I felt that if we could survive Holyrood then we could make it through anything.

BILL THOMSON, Former SPCB Assistant Chief Executive

I took on the role of Head of Implementation, where, alongside a very small team of four people, my job was to plan the move from the interim buildings into Holyrood. This was a challenging task. At that point, the Holyrood building was incomplete. There was a great deal of anger over the time it had taken and the cost. Therefore, those who had been in charge of the building process were understandably defensive about it, there was a bit of tension. But we needed information about when it would be ready, without which we couldn't plan the move. So, we had to develop an open working relationship with the people who had that information. We needed to get to know each other and develop a level of trust, to get to the point they were happy to share the information they had without worrying that we might misuse it.

But, the main constraint was that we had to achieve the move without a loss of parliamentary business. The only gap in proceedings that was long enough to achieve this was the summer recess – which was eight or nine weeks in length. The truth is, we initially thought it would happen in the summer of 2003. But the building wasn't ready, so it ended up being rescheduled for the following year. I had to trust the people I was working with that the building would be ready for the 2004 deadline. It would be wrong for me to say I never had any concerns that they wouldn't manage it, and we would be pushed back another year. But I was confident that it would work. In the end, everyone did what they were committed to doing, and we moved in during the summer of 2004 as planned. It wasn't just down to the four of us in the Implementation team, there was a lot of preparatory work done by all the offices in the Parliament and, indeed, by the elected members.

I felt incredible relief, and a real sense of satisfaction, after we completed the move. It made quite a difference to the whole institution. It was a turning point for perceptions of the Parliament, both among the public and those who worked here. The building was generally well received and was seen as a success. That meant that we attracted positive publicity. That in turn rubbed off onto those working here, who finally felt that they were working in an institution with a positive image. It made it a much happier place to be working at.

WILLIE HEIGH, SPCB Head of Project and Programme Management

When we moved in it was about relief more than anything else. It was exciting, but the occupation certificates were granted at something like three o'clock or four o'clock in the morning and we started moving people in at seven o'clock. It was pretty tough. I stayed overnight in the MacDonald Holyrood Hotel, got a few hours sleep, and came back in in the morning and thankfully we had managed to get our certificates in time to open up. I remember teams of guys all over the building just trying to get everything done. It was much tighter than what we experienced when we were refurbishing the temporary accommodation on The Mound. It was a different atmosphere altogether. But we got it done.

The folk working on it were conscious that the publicity had been so bad for the building that we had to make a success of the move, because it was a chance for a new start. George Reid was the Presiding Officer at the time and he was really behind us getting in and getting on. That was his mantra. We knew we had to make a success of it or else there would just be more trouble. There was a lot of plaudits and a lot of people were really happy with the accommodation when they saw it in person and not as a building site. I think there was more positivity after we were fully moved in and business was under way.

In terms of anecdotes, one of the craziest things that happened was when we were arranging with members who would be allocated to which office in the new Parliament building. It was still a building site, so you would bring them over and show them around. The top floor was the first one finished, we would take them up there and they would see the offices and think, 'This is lovely'. Downstairs was just like the worst building site you have ever been in. It was dark, there was no lights, there were puddles of water in places, so nobody wanted to be on the bottom floor. Agreeing where everybody would go felt like something out of *The Thick of It*, with things going on behind closed doors, party business managers talking to one another. We got there eventually but it was an eye-opener into how things happen at a political level. It's a bit smoother these days. There is more convention about who goes where, but I think they still have moments. I cannot begin to tell you how many different versions of the spreadsheet I had with different colours of each party on different floors and all the possible permutations. It was especially difficult then as well, because that was when we had the 'Rainbow Parliament'. You had the Greens, the SSP and five or six Independents. We had to try to fit that in with the major parties, and all of them wanted to go on the top floor and nobody wanting to go on the bottom floor. It was quite a time. We were at the Corporate Body for quite a few meetings and they could not agree it. It got to the point where I think it almost went to a vote of the Corporate Body, which is something that very rarely happens. But they eventually saw the writing on the wall and at the end of the day the Corporate Body members went to the business managers, they did whatever business managers do, and struck a deal. I would not like to say who the winners and losers out of all that were, but I think there was some political shenanigans went on and they agreed who would go where. It felt pretty severe at the time, and all over who got the nicest floor. It was very bizarre.

A New Building, a New Parliament?

The excitement of coming to Holyrood, and hope of turning a new page, is captured by Stephen Imrie and Ken Macintosh. Tricia Marwick contrasts the facilities on offer to those at the temporary accommodation, while the former Liberal Democrat MSP Jamie Stone compares them to Westminster, where he has served as an MP since 2017.

STEPHEN IMRIE, SPCB Clerk to the Justice Committee

I was desperate to move in. I really thought that bringing us all together into one place would help us. I felt we were very fragmented in the old site, and I honestly felt we weren't a real Parliament until we moved into the building. That was really the moment in time where it felt we were a proper Parliament. We had our own building and we were all together I was quite fed up at the negativity about it all, and that did impact on your morale. We were under the cosh. It seemed to be a lot of pressure and a lot of negativity, you just had to keep going. Looking back on it, the controversy about the cost and delays did affect staff morale, it definitely affected mine. But you just had to keep going, be professional, and you knew it would turn around.

After moving in, I thought we could move on from some of that negativity. I thought we could focus on what we were there for, which was holding the government to account, being the place people could come and bring views to the Parliament, we could do proper parliamentary work. That's what we're here for in a democracy. We could move on from the building, and the cost, and medals, and all of that side of things. I think we were doing it before, but some of the important work that was being done was just getting lost a bit in everything else. So, I thought moving into the building was a time to draw a line and move on, and I think staff were desperate to do that too, I certainly was.

KEN MACINTOSH, Presiding Officer and Former Labour Party MSP

The building is fantastic. It's quite a statement. I know not everyone likes it, but it really is a lovely building to work in. Both beautiful and very functional. It also played its part in the Parliament maturing, growing in strength and confidence. We had our own building, we had developed our own practices and we were no longer looking so much to what had gone before at Westminster and other legislatures. We began to take charge more. This was not just a result of the architecture itself, political changes have been instrumental too, but the building played its part in making the Parliament a far more confident institution.

TRICIA MARWICK, Former Presiding Officer and Scottish National Party MSP

Moving to Holyrood was fantastic. It was like night and day compared to the old site. Our offices at George IV Bridge were just the most horrible place. They were riddled with asbestos, they had to be knocked down after we moved out. Nobody had a room of their own, I was sharing a room with four other MSPs and four members of staff. You couldn't bring in members of the public to meet. The Holyrood building was full of light, with individual rooms, it made a huge difference. I think there was a lightening of our spirits once we went in. I have always loved the building. It made the Parliament itself seem more permanent. In the arrangements we had at the General Assembly and George IV Bridge, we didn't seem permanent. Every time the Church of Scotland held its General Assembly we had to move out. We moved out to Aberdeen one year, out to Glasgow another. The Parliament felt temporary in nature. That came to an end when we moved to Holyrood, we had a home of our own.

JAMIE STONE, Former Liberal Democrat MSP

The working environment in Holyrood is first class, in a lot of ways superior to Westminster. There's an advantage in being small. If you move around from A to B in Holyrood, the chances are you are going to bump into the relevant minister you are looking for. You will see them coming out of the chamber and say, 'Could I have a word with you?' I did that with Nicola Sturgeon when she was Health minister and I would say, 'What do you think about my new health centre?' I would have the chance to speak about it there and then. In Westminster, it is much more formal. There is a wariness about. They think, 'Who is this backbench-er?' It's not nearly as free and easy. You wouldn't necessarily just bump into the right person strolling about the place, it's too large. For instance, I've never bumped into Boris Johnson just strolling around. The layout of the building is conducive to that, it's very good. The garden lobby acts as a crossover. I think Enric Miralles designed it that way, so that you bump into each other as you go from A to B. Going to your office, or the chamber, or to get food, you're knocking into each other all the time.

Nostalgia for the Assembly Hall

Aspects of the Parliament's original home are warmly remembered in many corners. Alex Fergusson and Tavish Scott discuss the closeness they felt as MSPs between politics and the public there, while journalist Kirsten Camp-bell elaborates on the loss of an informal pub culture that came with the move to Holyrood and the consequences that had for the Parliament.

ALEX FERGUSSON, Former Presiding Officer and Conservative & Unionist Party MSP

I think it lost something when we moved to Holyrood. I loved it up the road, I loved the debating chamber. I thought the Church of Scotland's accommodation, because of the mixture of ancient and modern, was lovely. I loved the fact that you had to come out your office and walk 300 yards up the road, during which time people could line the streets and say, 'Who are you? I want to talk to you'. You were really close to the electorate. And they did do all sort of demonstrations. They used to line up for you coming out of decision time and you were within touching distance. I thought that was really good. We lost that down here. We've shut ourselves away a bit from that side of it. If you want to go and mix with people, you do it outside. You don't have to, you can come in through Queensberry House, or through the garage, and don't ever need to see anybody if you don't want to. Up there you had to. I thought that was a good idea. There is no doubt about it at all, politicians are less con-nected with the people here. Being screamed at when you're on your way to vote, or you're coming out and somebody goes, 'Here you, I want a word with you', that's good for you, keeps you honest. It was what we'd always promised, bringing politics closer to the people.

TAVISH SCOTT, Liberal Democrat MSP and Former Scottish Liberal Democrat Leader

In a practical sense, not a lot changed. We moved from one building to another. I liked our old home at the top of the Royal Mile. I thought we were close to the people. I never did like the Holyrood site, it is a 'sleepy hollow'. The building itself is fantastic, I love the architecture, it's a great place to work. But it isn't as embedded in Edinburgh, we are more secluded here. At our old home, people could demonstrate right outside of our window, they could grab you as you went across the street to vote. There were no hiding places. We are public servants, we earn a lot of money to do this job, we should be accountable to the people. All of that was lost when we came here, and there is more emphasis on security. Politics has become less accessible to the people because of that. There were some upsides to the, slightly frantic, arrangement at the top of the hill.

KIRSTEN CAMPBELL, BBC Scotland Political Journalist

The main thing that changed when we moved to Holyrood was the social side of things. It felt like you were rooted in Edinburgh at the temporary accommodation, rather than in a bubble. When we were up the road, there was a pub opposite the journalists' office called Deacon Brodie's, and it was a kind of unofficial gathering place for the Parliament. Each party had their own pub, the SNP would go to the Jinglin' Geordies, the Tories would go to the Bow Bar, the Lib Dems had somewhere further down. But if something big happened, if somebody had resigned, or that important piece of legislation passed, then people tended to congregate in Deacon Brodie's. You did a lot of gossiping and a lot of chatting, there was a lot of cross-party engagement in the pub. When we moved down here, you were a bit out of it. There aren't really any bars that you could get to easily, or if you did then not everybody would know where it was. There is a bar in the building, but it hasn't worked in the same way.

Originally, journalists were banned from it. I was the treasurer of the Scottish Parliamentary Journalists Association at the time, we had been around all of the party group meetings speaking to them about the importance of good relations between politicians and journalists and the ability to socialise. But some MSPs were concerned that they might be talking about politically sensitive matters, or they might be speaking to constituents, and they didn't want journalists eavesdropping. There had been a couple of occasions where ministers had lost jobs because they said something unguarded in front of a journalist who then reported it around that time, so there was a bit of sensitivity about. Regardless, they banned us from the bar and we weren't allowed in. That was eventually overturned, and they let the journalists in. But it was too late. By that point, the habit had gone. People didn't use the bar. I think in part because the journalists didn't go, which can be useful for politicians. The whole atmosphere changed as a result, it lost that vibe and the social side worsened.

Parliamentary Culture

Old Scars and a New Stage

As the Scottish Parliament moved beyond its tumultuous first years, and got used to its new residence at Holyrood, the culture of the institution was changing. Willie Heigh, David McGill and Mary-Ann Masson recall the development of a skittishness when it came to spending and any hint of media criticism. This represented one of the clearest scars that the controversies of the early days had left behind on the institution and the staff working within it. It was an effort to shelter a still fragile Parliament from harm, but remained with the Parliament long after it had become a more entrenched part of Scottish society, that no longer needed the same degree of protection. Andrew Mylne comments on the end of the Parliament's pioneering period, and the beginning of a more settled era. Its processes and structures were now increasingly established, and the prospects of fast-moving changes with little bureaucratic oversight were becoming a thing of the past.

WILLIE HEIGH, SPCB Head of Project and Programme Management

In the early years after we moved in I do not think they could spend money on anything without getting criticised. That made doing any work difficult. You were constantly talking to the Media Office to get what the media angle will be on this. We would buy some new furniture, basic things any organisation has to do, but were constantly thinking about how it would go down in the press. I would not say you were worrying about these things constantly, because even when it was at its worst you would generally get on with doing the job, but you were always conscious of the way things might go over. That is not a good place for any organisation to be in. I think as time has gone on and we have become mature as an institution, we probably know better than to react on that kind of stuff but the press are no longer really interested in that anymore anyway. They have much bigger fish to fry nowadays. That sort of press scrutiny probably started to wane a wee bit by the 2007 election. It has been quite settled for a while now. It has taken its time, but we got there.

DAVID McGILL, SPCB Assistant Chief Executive

We became very risk averse very quickly. We were always thinking of how things were going to be perceived by the press and the public. We were conscious of what we could say, and what we couldn't. Often, we had good ideas kicking around that were complete non-starters because we were worried we would get roasted in the papers because of them. That culture may well have been a result of the Holyrood building controversy. But, it is something that many other public sector organisations deal with. We are always very exposed to criticism for our spending, it is something we can often agonise over, when perhaps it would be better to just toughen up and move forward.

MARY-ANN MASSON, SPCB Internal Communications Manager

People were quite bruised from the media coverage around the building. I didn't join the Parliament until 2004, at the end of that process, so didn't carry the same level of baggage as some of the other staff. It had been a difficult process; a lot of senior people had been under attack by the press. The impact I saw coming out of all of that was a lot of nervousness about what we put into print about anything. I produced the Corporate Bulletin, which comes out once a week and keeps people updated on the goings on in the Parliament. We used to have to be so careful about what we put in that, in case it was passed on to the press and became a negative story. The scrutiny that we were under was very intense. That was magnified in 2006 when the beam came down in the debating chamber. We went into crisis mode and had to step up to deal with what was going on. That was a very stressful time. In some ways it took us back to the sense of adversity we had over the building process.

ANDREW MYLNE, SPCB Clerk Team Leader

When I took over the Procedures Committee in session two there were still a number of quite big problems that had been identified and hadn't been fixed. If you look back at the Standing Orders now, a lot of the bigger changes that have been made since 1999 were made in session two. In session one, it had all been slightly overwhelming and there had been so much to do that we hadn't had the chance to deal with the issues that had been identified. This was the chance to fix them. By the time we got to session three and later, most of the work had been done and everything had settled down a lot more. There's less pressure to make changes now. I think it's inevitable that the Parliament would reach this point, I don't see how an institution can avoid it. It's not necessarily a bad thing: you don't want permanent revolution, you need a degree of continuity. If you have developed effective working practice that balance the various interests that are involved, and you've got some precedent behind that, then it is actually a good thing. It's like having an effective working piece of machinery. If it works, if it's not broke, don't fix it. You should always be alert to the possibility that you can do things differently, and be prepared to meet people from other places and look with an open mind at what they do. We should always be open to that. But if we've got to the stage where most of our practices largely work the way we think that they should, we shouldn't feel the need to constantly change things. I think it is getting that balance. Inevitably, the Parliament will become more set in its ways, the rate of change will continue to slow down overall. But we do live in an uncertain political environment, and new challenges are always coming along. So, we always have to maintain that willingness to look at things afresh.

The Parliamentary Expenses Scandal

The parliamentary expenses scandal challenged public faith in politics and politicians across the United Kingdom during the 2000s. In 2005, the Freedom of Information (Scotland) Act came into force. It made it possible for individuals to request previously private information from public organisations. Quickly, enquiries started to come in regarding the expenses that parliamentarians claimed from the public purse. In Westminster, the disclosure of this information was resisted for years. Disdain for the political class grew as a result, culminating in an angry response when the details of MPs', sometimes suspect, expenses claims finally became public in 2009. As Paul Grice notes, the Scottish Parliament took a different approach. Expenses data was released in full at an early point in the affair. While Holyrood didn't escape the wider backlash against politicians, Grice credits the Parliament's handling of the scandal with strengthening its position.

PAUL GRICE, SPCB Clerk and Chief Executive

The expenses scandal down south was the stand out issue of the rest of the second session, after we had moved into Holyrood. It was really a massive focus for us. We never had the scandal up here, but clearly we were affected by it. After the Freedom of Information (Scotland) Act had come in, releasing members' expenses became our top priority. George Reid was wonderfully knowledgeable about what he called 'public affairs' and had great instincts on the issue. With his political strength, and hopefully a bit of know-how on my side, we managed to get this institution through that without there being a scandal. There simply wasn't one in Scotland. We were on top of it from a very early point. The members hadn't been at it in any sense, we ran a much tighter regime here, but it wasn't the most popular thing when we decided that we were going to publish their expenses. There were a lot of fraught discussions, and we had to persuade a lot of people. I got great political support for that from George and the Corporate Body of the day. When we said that we were going to publish all of this information it ultimately helped us. Bearing in mind that the Parliament's reputation was not good after the Holyrood project, by avoiding a scandal we were able to build confidence.

The Rainbow Parliament

Session two, running from 2003 to 2007, is widely remembered as the 'Rainbow Parliament'. The 2003 election had seen small parties and Independents take advantage of the poor performance of Labour and the SNP to dramatically increase their representation. The Greens won seven seats, the SSP six, the Senior Citizens Unity Party one, and Independents three. Over the course of the next four years, their numbers grew further, as Campbell Martin of the SNP and Brian Monteith of the Conservatives left their parties and began sitting as Independents. These successes, meant that both the Greens and SSP, and following defections the Independent MSPs as well, were entitled to a seat on the Parliamentary Bureau for the first time after meeting the requirements of having five members. This is an important body within the Parliament, with a significant influence over the way business is carried out. By gaining access to it, the smaller parties had a real opportunity to shape the way politics was conducted in the Parliament. Yet, the flourishing of these groups was very short lived. At the next election in 2007, the Socialists and Senior Citizens' Unity Party lost all of their seats, the Greens were reduced to two and just one Independent was returned. At no other point have the major parties been nearly as weak as they were between 2003 and 2007, while the Parliament has never come close to housing the same diversity of political views. The situation that held during that session challenged many of the Parliament's existing structures, which had largely been designed to accommodate the traditional parties rather than these newcomers, and had to adjust accordingly. The results were even more transformational for the parties themselves, with the Greens and SSP both advancing from the status of one-man bands to become burgeoning parliamentary groups. This step up carried many opportunities and problems that both were forced to confront.

Neil Stewart and Ken Hughes, alongside the Independent MSP Dennis Canavan, detail the ways in which the Parliament's processes adapted to the new situation, and addressed some of the challenges the 'Rainbow Parliament' presented. Tommy Sheridan of the Socialists and Robin Harper of the Greens describe the impact of their parties' transitions from single-MSP organisations to substantial groups, and the difficulties that arose as a result.

The New Parties

NEIL STEWART, SPCB Senior Assistant Clerk

There was an acknowledgement that many of the Independents and members of small parties elected in 2003 didn't have an established party structure behind them to help induct them into the Parliament. We felt that every member ought to be given the requisite tools to do their job properly. John Swinburne of the Senior Citizens' Unity Party and the newly elected Independent Jean Turner were probably identified as having specific needs. Margo MacDonald and Dennis Canavan had been here in the first session, and the Greens and SSP had some support as party groups in their own right. But John and Jean were brand new, had come from non-political backgrounds and did not have any kind of party machine behind them. On a personal level, people like myself were encouraged to take more of an interest to help them. I was working on the Chamber Desk at the time, which was probably one of their main interfaces with parliamentary staff and the Parliament, so I just gave them more time to talk over what motions were, what parliamentary questions involved, how the debate system worked, how to vote in the chamber, how everything fitted together. There was an encouragement from senior management to invest time in helping them get on with their jobs. There was also an acknowledgement that with the Greens and SSP doing well that year, there was a whole group of new MSPs coming from a non-parliamentary background that needed a bit more help from the start. But I looked out for Jean and John in particular. So we didn't make any formal change to our structures to accommodate these new members, we just acknowledged that there was a need for a little extra support.

KEN HUGHES, SPCB Assistant Chief Executive

In 2003, we had the 'Rainbow Parliament'. The vote for both Labour and SNP had gone down, and it was the Greens and SSP who had hoovered them up, along with a sprinkling of Independents and the Senior Citizens' Unity Party. So, we had this broader base of political interest. This was represented in the Parliamentary Bureau, because you can't have representation in the Bureau unless you have five or more MSPs. But the Greens and SSP had more than five, and the Independents and Senior Citizens eventually got the numbers after a defection to get a seat on the Bureau as well.

All of a sudden, you had quite a different spread of political interest across parliamentary structures. That made us think about how we managed debates, how we allocated people's right to ask questions at First Minister's Questions. If it had been done solely on proportion, these smaller groups wouldn't get a look in. But we knew that the Parliament should be totally cross-party and not exclusive. So, we had to think of ways of giving these smaller parties more say than they would have been entitled to on a solely mathematical basis. We had to think in a far broader way than we had in the first session of how to include these voices.

We didn't look at examples from other countries of how smaller parties were handled. We spoke to the parties themselves and asked what they expected to do. I can always remember Tommy Sheridan, he was a lone gunman in the first session but in the second had five others around him. He maintained that this gave him the entitlement to a seat on the front bench. In the first few sittings of the Parliament he took a seat on the front bench. I spoke to other parties to decide where they would sit in the chamber. In the end he was only dissuaded from sitting there after the Labour MSP Duncan McNeil, an ex-boilermaker and rather sturdy individual, got in the chamber first and sat in Tommy Sheridan's seat, thus convincing Tommy not to sit there.

In the middle of that session, the SSP staged a protest in the middle of FMQs, in the run-up to the G8 summit at Gleneagles. In the middle of FMQs, they rushed to the front of the chamber and stopped parliamentary business in protest. We advised the Presiding Officer to suspend business, because we couldn't go on. We didn't have a procedure to manage the situation. We couldn't do anything about it. We had to wait until they left. It was the sort of thing you wouldn't have expected to happen in parliaments with a different sort of makeup.

DENNIS CANAVAN, Former Independent MSP

After the 2003 election, the Scottish Socialist Party and the Scottish Green Party had enough MSPs to get recognition on the Parliamentary Bureau. At that time, you needed five members to be recognised. Of the rest, there was of course Margo MacDonald, elected in 2003 as an Independent, Dr Jean Turner who was elected as an Independent, and John Swinburne, who wasn't an Independent but was the only member elected for the Scottish Senior Citizens' Unity Party. So, there were just the four of us. We weren't large enough to get representation on the Bureau. If memory serves, after that an SNP MSP Campbell Martin had a disagreement with his leadership and he had the whip withdrawn to become an Independent. That meant that we had five in our group and could get representation on the Parliamentary Bureau. Margo was our representative, and was excellent at it. As a Lothian MSP she could be based at the Parliament all the time, and always spoke up on behalf of our small group. Her activity made us more influential, and gave us a fairer kick of the ball. I think the

Parliament needs the diversity of views that we brought, and lost something when most of the Independents lost their seats in 2007.

TOMMY SHERIDAN, Former Scottish Socialist Party and Solidarity Convener and MSP

The SSP became a more serious proposition for a lot of people after the 2003 election. It was a fantastic achievement to get six members elected, and two in Glasgow. However, it brought more tension than we had before. Up until then, I had a close-knit team in the Parliament. I had an office manager, I had a press officer and I had me. We worked really well as a team, and we did as much as we could. Then we had five other personalities coming in, all of whom had their own way of doing things. Personality clashes developed quickly. I remember in one of our first group meetings, one of the members came back with a form to fill in that she was quite angry about. In order to become registered as a part of the Corporate Body in the Parliament, you had to state the leader of the party. She said, 'I'm going to put your name down, but I've told them you're not the leader, you're only the Convener'. I should have realised then that this was going to be the beginning of a rough ride. All of a sudden taking initiatives became harder, because every decision had to be discussed and agreed by committee. Whereas before I felt like I had free reign to campaign on the issues I thought were important, and were in line with the SSP manifesto, I felt more constrained in the second session.

ROBIN HARPER, Former Scottish Green Party MSP and Co-convener

The second session was amazing. It was a bit difficult at the beginning. In the first session, my team had been largely self-organised and acted relatively independently. We got slightly carried away at the idea of being a larger party from 2003, and we tried to develop all the structures you need as a larger party very quickly. There were some unnecessary tensions within the group because we were so keen to be seen as completely professional from the first. We might have been better off taking things more easily, allowing them to develop organically rather than trying to invent a whole system on short notice. There were a lot of new people coming in, both MSPs and their staff, to bed in.

But the expansion of our party gave us a lot more publicity. We were invited to speak on the radio and television more often, we got our viewpoints into the newspapers. We had more of a handle on things. It also gave me more freedom to pursue the things I was interested in.

Previously, I had done anything and everything to try to keep the Green Party in the public eye. It was a conscious choice to go for profile as much as possible. That involved a lot of travelling around the country, and that took up a lot of my time. Now people had their own areas to represent. I was then able to concentrate more on the core Green political issues I cared about the most.

The SSP–Solidarity Split

While the Scottish Parliament has seen a number of MSPs leave the party under whose label they were elected, and even join new ones, it has only seen one of its parties split into two. That was when two members of the SSP group left to form Solidarity in 2006. Internal relations within the SSP parliamentary group had fallen apart in the midst of bitterness relating to the conduct of the party's former Convener and most recognisable public figure, Tommy Sheridan, during his legal dispute with the *News of the World* newspaper. Once they had reached an unreconcilable point, Sheridan and one other SSP MSP, Rosie Byrne, left to form their own party, leaving behind a rump SSP group of four.

Tommy Sheridan takes the chance to describe the practical process of forming this new group mid-session, and the consequences the split had for both his own influence and that of his former SSP colleagues in the Parliament.

TOMMY SHERIDAN, Former Scottish Socialist Party and Solidarity Convener and MSP

When the split between the Scottish Socialist Party and Solidarity occurred in 2006, we had to re-register with the Corporate Body and nominate a leader and co-leader for Solidarity, myself and Rosemary Byrne. The SSP also had to re-register because they went from six to four MSPs. That was probably the most straightforward part of the process. Getting office space was a bit more problematic. Many of our differences were personal rather than political. Major personal antagonism had developed. So it would have been better for Solidarity to move to a different part of the building, but that wasn't possible because of the restrictions

Scottish Parliamentary Corporate Body Staff, 1999.

Group photo of 32 female MSPs in the Black and White Corridor of the temporary home of the Parliament on The Mound to mark International Women's Day, March 2002.

Sir David Steel and Paul Grice, Clerk and Chief Executive of the Scottish Parliament, at the Scottish Parliament Roadshow in the Elphinstone Hall, Aberdeen, May 2002.

The Chamber of the Parliament on The Mound, June 2002.

Scottish Socialist Party MSP Rosie Kane, May 2003.

Paul Grice, Clerk and Chief Executive of the Scottish Parliament, explains features of a new MSP office to *Edinburgh Evening News* editor Ian Stewart and *Scotland on Sunday* editor John McLellan in the MSP block of the Holyrood building, June 2003.

Sir David Steel finds MSP David McLetchie's reflection of his time as the Scottish Parliament's Presiding Officer amusing, June 2003.

Jack McConnell, John Swinney, David McLetchie, Jim Wallace and Robin Harper await the arrival of Her Majesty the Queen in the Black and White Corridor of the temporary home of the Parliament on The Mound, June 2003.

Sir Sean Connery visiting the new Scottish Parliament site at Holyrood, August 2003.

The new Scottish Parliament building at Holyrood, October 2003.

Clerk and Chief Executive Paul Grice welcoming SPCB staff to the new Scottish Parliament complex. The staff gathered in the new debating chamber for the first time, August 2004.

View from Salisbury Crags of the new Scottish Parliament at Holyrood, September 2004.

Interior of the Debating Chamber showing the oak and steel beam roof at the Scottish Parliament complex, 2005.

Two figures look over a snow covered Holyrood complex, with Queensberry House and the Committee Towers in view from Calton Hill, February 2005.

Scottish Socialist Party protest in the Debating Chamber of the Scottish Parliament, June 2005. This protest and occupation of the Chamber resulted in a meeting of the Standards Committee which decided to suspend the members involved from Parliament for one month without pay,.

Members of the public wait on Horse Wynd to enter the Scottish Parliament during the first Doors Open Day to be held at the Scottish Parliament complex, September 2005.

The long queue for the first Doors Open Day to be held at the Scottish Parliament snakes its way up the Royal Mile, September, 2005.

Bashir Ahmed MSP is sworn in as a Member of the Scottish Parliament, May 2007.

The 15th Duke of Hamilton, accompanied by his son Alexander Douglas Douglas-Hamilton, processes the Crown of Scotland into the Parliament ahead of Her Majesty the Queen's arrival, July 2007, the last occasion that the 15th Duke of Hamilton carried out this ceremonial role.

Queen Elizabeth II departs the Chamber to the Black and White Corridor, accompanied by Presiding Officer Alex Fergusson, following the session three opening ceremony. The Royal Archers and Persuivants line the corridor, July 2007.

First Minister Alex Salmond MSP, Jack McConnell MSP, Annabel Goldie MSP and Nicol Stephen MSP wait to meet Her Majesty the Queen in the Garden Lobby during the Royal Opening of session three of the Scottish Parliament, July 2007.

The Scottish Parliament pictured from Salisbury Crags in November 2010, as Edinburgh experiences the deepest November snowfall for 17 years. An estimated 10 inches of snow fell over the weekend. Calton Hill and Regent Road can be seen in the background.

Nigel Don MSP convenes a meeting of the Subordinate Legislation Committee in Committee Room Six. Committee members John Scott, John Pentland, Michael McMahon and Mike Mackenzie are pictured, January 2012.

Donald Trump, Chairman and Chief Executive Officer of the Trump Organization, gives evidence to the Scottish Parliament's Economy Energy and Tourism Committee during its inquiry into the Scottish Government's renewable energy targets, April 2012.

Members of the media watch on as Donald Trump, Chairman and Chief Executive Officer of the Trump Organization, gives a press conference with the Scottish Parliament's Economy Energy and Tourism Committee, April 2012.

Scottish Parliament staff who volunteered to assist at the 2014 Commonwealth Games in Glasgow pictured outside the Scottish Parliament on Horse Wynd, July 2014.

Group photo of session five Members of the Scottish Parliament, May 2016.

Her Majesty Queen Elizabeth II meets with party leaders at the opening of the Scottish Parliament, June 2016.

(L–R) Lord David Steel, Sir George Reid, Tricia Marwick, and Sir Alex Fergusson. The four former Presiding Officers of the Scottish Parliament, at the opening of session five of the Scottish Parliament, July 2016.

Presiding Officer Ken Macintosh MSP and Clerk and Chief Executive Paul Grice present an award to James Brown upon completion of his Modern Apprenticeship Programme at the Scottish Parliament, November 2016.

Presiding Officer Ken Macintosh MSP, who was joined by fellow MSPs and Clerk and Chief Executive Paul Grice on a fact finding visit to RAF Lossimouth, July 2017.

Clerk and Chief Executive Paul Grice and Assistant Chief Executive David McGill are given a tour of the Parliament's Committee Tower roofs by high level access and maintenance contractors TRAC, December 2017.

on the Parliament's office space. That meant that the two parties' offices ended up being cheek by jowl. Sometimes we were literally next door, because we both shared a meeting room that had previously been for the whole of the SSP to use. We would sometimes pass each other coming in and out. That was very difficult, because by this time personal relationships had entirely broken down. They didn't have any time for us and we didn't have any time for them.

The split also impacted upon our privileges in the Parliament. Each party that is registered with the Corporate Body gets a share of short money, a budget to spend on research, PR, administrative support and things like that. We had previously qualified for it, but now neither the SSP or Solidarity had enough MSPs. It had to be cut from both parties and I think we qualified for something very limited. Up until then, we had negotiated with the Parliament that every second week we would be guaranteed a question during First Minister's Questions. I thought I had utilised that very well. I saw it as an opportunity to say things that others were not saying and I relished the chance to take on the First Minister. After the split, I only had the chance to have a question every four or six weeks. That was undermining. But frankly, we had already been undermined by the whole split anyway.

Ethnic Minorities in the Scottish Parliament

Scotland has a much smaller ethnic minority population than the rest of the United Kingdom, with the minorities making up more than three times as great a proportion the English population as they do Scotland's. Yet, even accounting for these demographic differences, the Scottish Parliament has fallen desperately short of adequately representing this part of the country.

The first non-white MSP was not elected until 2007, when Bashir Ahmed won his seat. The community was again left completely unrepresented after Ahmed tragically died from a heart attack in 2009, only two years into his tenure. In all, there have been just four non-white MSPs, Bashir Ahmed and Humza Yousaf of the SNP, and Labour's Hanzala Malik and Anas Sarwar. All of them have come from the Asian community, and have represented Glasgow in the Parliament.

Humza Yousaf, who worked in Bashir Ahmed's office before being elected as an MSP in his own right in 2011, discusses the weight of responsibility he felt towards his community and the way in which this shaped his activities as a politician with a wide range of interests and ambitions for the whole of Scotland.

HUMZA YOUSAF, Scottish National Party MSP

If you remember the 2007 election, the SNP won it by one seat. It was all marginal, we got the result of that final seat at one in the afternoon the day after the election and by three that same day I had been offered a job to work with Bashir Ahmad MSP, who had just been elected as the first non-white MSP, as his office manager. Bashir Ahmad passed away mid-term on 6 February 2009. After that, there was again no ethnic minority member of the Scottish Parliament. This Parliament was all white, and that's not a representation of our nation by any stretch. So I was convinced to stand at the next election in 2011. I got second on the SNP's Glasgow list, just behind Nicola Sturgeon, and I was elected. I felt a very heavy sense of responsibility that I didn't feel as a parliamentary assistant as soon as I entered into this Parliament.

I made the decision very early on that I was going to take the oath of the Parliament in both Urdu and English. I wanted to have that reflected in the Parliament. I felt a real responsibility to both my region, Glasgow, but also to the Scottish Pakistani community. I knew they were going to be watching closely, because they were really proud of me. I got lots of messages on the day I got elected. I even got a message from the mayor of my dad's hometown in Pakistan, a tiny town called Mian Channu which very few people have heard of. He phoned me up on the day after polling and said, 'I read about you in the news and we heard about you and it's great, we're having a celebration here as you're one of our own'. This institution really took on a whole different meaning for me once I got elected.

I felt a responsibility as one of the only ethnic minority members. But, if I am being honest, I think I probably did myself and that community a little bit of a disservice in that I probably overcompensated. I never wanted to be the brown guy talking about racism, I never want to be pigeonholed as the ethnic minority that just spoke about racism. So, I think I purposely distanced myself from making sure that I didn't talk about it too much. I probably overcompensated, because it should have been an opportunity to talk more about this issue. But I chose not to. I think on reflection that was the wrong thing to do. I didn't have much time to get into these kinds of backbench campaigns, because I was elected in May 2011 and by September of 2012 I was asked to be in government. So, I didn't have much time as a backbencher to maybe raise these issues more. I think I'm in a much better place, a much more confident place, to speak on these matters now. Hopefully, I represent the people of Pollok well on a daily basis in this place, but also there's an added responsibility not just to the Scottish Pakistani community but most minorities, who look towards both myself and the only other ethnic minority MSP, Anas Sarwar, to raise their issues in the Parliament.

List and Regional MSPs

One of the quirks of the Scottish Parliament's additional member electoral system was the introduction of two separate categories of MSP. These were the 73 members elected to represent constituencies, and the 59 elected from regional party lists. Both types of MSPs were in theory entirely equal, with the same voting rights, pay scales and privileges as parliamentarians. However, constituency MSPs bear a substantially greater workload, with constituency casework taking up a much larger portion of their time than list MSPs are confronted with. However, being a constituency MSP has, from the birth of the Parliament, been seen as a source of great prestige that almost all MSPs have strived to attain. In the early days of the Parliament, the differences between the two types of MSP were particularly stark, with those elected on the list being seen as a lower-grade politician in some quarters.

At times, there were very pronounced tensions between list and constituency members. List MSPs often used their platform as parliamentarians to extensively target constituency seats, sparking off intense animosity from the threatened incumbents. These issues have partially eased over time. Greater familiarity with the system has certainly helped, but the changing political context has also been important. There are now many MSPs who have served in both roles. In particular, a number of former list MSPs in the SNP have subsequently won constituency seats, and often hold senior roles, while several former constituency MSPs in the Labour Party have since been elected on the list. Nonetheless, the hierarchy between the two types of MSP has never been entirely pushed aside by the passage of time.

Three members to have served in both roles explore these questions. The former SNP MSP Tricia Marwick comments on the perception of list MSPs as being second-tier politicians during the early days of the Parliament, and Linda Fabiani observes the differences in workloads for the two types of members. The Conservative Jackson Carlaw then goes into greater detail, observing the more localised perspective available to constituency MSPs and the stronger personal connection they are able to build with their constituencies.

TRICIA MARWICK, Former Presiding Officer and Scottish National Party MSP

If you were a list MSP in the early days it was just awful. We were second class citizens. While we might have got the same pay, it was quite clear that the government of the day thought that we were lesser beings than constituency members. I can remember meetings in which I was told I could only attend if a constituency MSP was invited along as well. Meanwhile, if a constituency MSP had a meeting with the government on an issue I had also been working on, I was never invited. That's changed, but at the beginning we were very much left to feel like second class citizens. I think the change was partly a result of the SNP coming into government in 2007. It showed a far greater willingness to work with MSPs regardless of their status, many of the SNP members being list MSPs themselves. We saw quite a difference from 2007 onwards.

LINDA FABIANI, Scottish National Party MSP

If you're in opposition, what you want to do is capture a constituency seat. That's how our system works. Regardless of how much we talk about parity between regional MSPs and list MSPs, there is still something in our psyche that says that you have got to win the constituency. As a list MSP, you shadow a particular seat that you think you could gain advantage and look for opportunities. If you're shadowing a seat, you do pick up some constituency work. But it is nothing to the extent that you do as a constituency MSP, where it is constant and you never get on top of it. So as a list MSP you are able to have particular interests across your region, or nationally, or indeed internationally. You can pursue these things, like I did as I went into international development and human rights. You do not have the time to pursue them as a constituency MSP. I have found it just impossible to do any of that. It was a whole new challenge after I won my seat, it was like a completely new job.

JACKSON CARLAW, Conservative & Unionist Party MSP

The roles of being a regional and constituency MSP are both equally fascinating. Being elected as a regional member gives you responsibility for a vast territory. My region in the West of Scotland was vast, that allowed for me to sometimes see the big picture in a way that a constituency member cannot. For example, a constituency member may be aware of how the policies of the health board are affecting a section of their own constituency or certain individual constituents. But, at times I became aware that a policy was having an impact on a whole different series of communities and people. When you saw it over a whole territory and in different places you started to realise it was a much bigger issue. So sometimes I think you were alerted to quite big issues in a way that as a constituency member you might not have picked up on, because it might not have affected that many people in your own area and you therefore might have thought it was quite a minor concern.

Casework was much more sporadic as a regional member, because I think instinctively people associate the immediate concern they have as something they take to their local constituency MP or MSP. So there was a very considerable uplift in the constituency casework compared to being a regional member. I know from some colleagues in other parties who've gone from being constituency to regional members that the constituency casework stopped after they changed roles, even though they'd been the constituency member beforehand. It just dropped off dramatically. So that has been a considerable shift. I've welcomed that because actually, it has proved to be a fresh dynamic and challenge for me. I had been in the Parliament for nine years as a regional member, and suddenly I was now doing and exploring casework on behalf of constituents in a much more structured way than I did before. So it presented a different challenge.

It has also been very important to me personally to win a constituency seat. I was born in my constituency, Eastwood. I was born in what is now a hotel that used to be a maternity home. Gordon Brown, the former Prime Minister, was born on the same maternity ward. I'd always had an ambition to one day represent the people in the community in which I'd been born, grown up, lived and brought my family up in. It did feel different the night I was elected. Coming back from Parliament the week after I was sworn in, and sort of subconsciously thinking I'm coming back to my constituency was quite an emotional feeling in a way that travelling back to a huge region like the West of Scotland as one of several regional members could not be. You are equally proud to be a member of Parliament, but there is a different connection. But it was a more superficial connection with the region than you have with a more manageable entity. In a constituency, you really know every street and every shop and every community centre and you get to know many of the personalities and see them repeatedly over the piece. So it's quite a different thing. It meant a lot.

Changing of the Guard

The 2007 election was one of the clearest turning points in the nation's political history. Not only did it see the government that had run the Scottish Executive since the advent of devolution in 1999 lose power, it cleared away many of the certainties of Scottish politics that had held for decades. Prior to the contest, the Labour Party had won every Parliamentary election in Scotland, at both Westminster and the Scottish Parliament, since 1959. At its peak in the late 1980s and 1990s its position appeared insurmountable. For Labour to be reduced to opposition and the SNP to be thrust into government office for the first time in their history, marked a historic change. In the years since the SNP's razor thin victory in 2007, they have definitively replaced Labour as Scotland's leading party. They have controlled the Scottish Government as either a minority or majority administration for the past 12 years, winning re-election in 2011 and 2016. They also won the majority of Scottish seats at the 2015 and 2017 UK general elections, with Labour's success in the 2010 Westminster contest standing out as the SNP's only defeat in a nationwide Parliamentary election since 2007.

Minority Government 2007–2011

The 2007 election produced an incredibly tight balance within the Parliament. The SNP had just one seat more than their nearest rivals in the Labour Party, and just over a third of the seats in the chamber overall.

This meant that they could only pass legislation through building broad alliances with different parties on an issue-by-issue basis, and could see their government brought down at any time if the opposition parties joined together to vote them out. In comparison to the coalition that had preceded it, and the Westminster majority governments that the British public were most familiar with, this situation was extremely fragile. With the government's fate out of its own hands, few expected the SNP to see out the entire session. Many were concerned that Scotland would be ungovernable, and that the Parliament would be overly strained. These fears were eventually proven unfounded. Although the government was beaten on a number of issues, and came very close to falling after its budget proposals were initially voted down in 2009, the SNP minority remained in place through its full four-year term. Indeed, some saw this session as the closest the Parliament has ever come to achieving the consensus-driven 'new politics' envisioned by its founders. Certainly, it marked a high point in the level of cross-party collaboration, and the power of the Parliament's opposition parties to effect change on the government. The contrast with later sessions has been stark.

David McGill points to some of the concerns members of the SPCB had in 2007 about the prospect of minority government. The politics of the period are then discussed by some of the key participants in these years. Alex Fergusson describes how he approached this session as Presiding Officer, and the willingness he found among all parties to work together. Robin Harper recalls the important role the Green Party's two MSPs played, describing the confidence and supply agreement they reached with the SNP and their subsequent role in bringing the government to the brink of collapse during the budget negotiations in 2009. The SNP's Alex Neil and John Swinney, both government ministers in these years, delve into the practicalities of running a minority administration from the position of relative weakness their party held.

DAVID MCGILL, SPCB Assistant Chief Executive

After the 2007 election, one of the things we worried about was getting overloaded. We had a government that claimed a mandate to get its policies through after finishing as the largest party, and an opposition that could say that it had only fallen one seat short and was going to pursue its own policies. At that point, we thought that we could end up with two programmes for government. We were really worried about getting swamped. We wondered whether our structures were going to fall apart under the pressure, and how our existing rules could stand up to minority government.

In the end, the Parliament coped very well. There were a few changes that we needed to make. But most of them were focused on protocol and the administrative side of things rather than parliamentary rules. The parliamentary rules actually stood up extremely well to those unprecedented results. I think that was because of the personalities involved. There was a maturity among the politicians that we hadn't anticipated. The government's business manager took an active role in dealing with his opposites in the other parties and conveying the government's position. He took responsibility for building relationships, building coalitions on an issue by issues basis and seeking to make things work. What could have been a really difficult session worked pretty well.

ALEX FERGUSSON, Former Presiding Officer and Conservative & Unionist Party MSP

I think we only had one parliamentary session of the new style of politics in action, which was the period when I was Presiding Officer, from 2007 to 2011. This was because we had a minority government and the numbers in the Parliament meant that the Scottish Government had to find different partners and different coalitions on every vote to get anything passed. I believe very strongly that the Parliament as an institution was at its most effective in its scrutiny role and committees were at their most effective because government didn't have a majority on them either. When you contrast it with the years when we did have a majority government, I don't think they compare. It was made to work by both the opposition and government alike.

It was fascinating having a minority government, but in a way it made my job as Presiding Officer easier. There was constant dialogue between the parties and the party business managers. Sometimes it took place in the Presiding Officer's office. But very rarely did it come down to me having to bash heads together. There were a couple of occasions when things broke down, with moments like when I had to vote down the budget because the vote in the chamber was tied. You don't do that lightly. But there was a willingness on all sides to make that period work. And I think that willingness saw it through. But it was a fascinating time to be chairing the Parliament, no doubt about it.

ROBIN HARPER, Former Scottish Green Party MSP and Co-convener

We were put in a position where we could have left the SNP to seek support from the Conservatives whenever there was anything particularly contentious in the chamber and hope other parties abstained, or we could get a small amount of influence by going into a confidence and supply arrangement ourselves. We spent two days up at St Andrews House with the civil servants, and with Patrick Harvie locked in an office with John Swinney, and came up with an agreement. We wanted to make sure that we did not give the public the idea that we were linked solidly with the SNP. We had disagreements from the start, over the Edinburgh trams, which we supported and they opposed, and the new Forth Road Bridge, which we opposed and they supported. When it came to signing the agreement, Alex Salmond wanted a photograph outside with me for the press. I said to my team that that was fine, but I did not want a photograph of me shaking Alex Salmond's hand, because that would look as if we were buddy-buddies – which we were not. If we got into that kind of situation, we could have been very badly damaged. So, on the day I clutched a big green file in my right hand and I said, 'Tell him I'm not shaking hands'. That made it obvious to Alex that we meant it.

The next year, we wanted a substantial sum of money in the budget for insulation of the poorest houses in Scotland, mostly poor condition council housing. I can't remember the sum of money they offered us, but it was derisory. It was in the thousands rather than the millions. So, we announced that we were going to be voting against the budget. That would have swung it. The Liberal Democrats and Labour were never going to vote for that budget. The Conservatives were, because the SNP had been clever enough to produce a budget that the Conservatives would support. It was last minute stuff. The SNP came back with a hugely increased bid. Patrick and I said, 'That's nice, but where is this money coming from? Can you tell us how you managed to get this amount of money out of the budget?' They couldn't explain it. I thought, 'You haven't done your sums up here. This has just been plucked out of the sky'. So we put the budget down. The sky didn't fall in on everybody, because what happens in any government in that situation is that the original budget for the previous year carries on operating, the same amount of money per project as the previous year until the budget is worked out.

As a result of what we did, Labour got a sweetener, the Liberals got a sweetener, the Conservatives got a sweetener and we lost even that which we had. There was no money provided, which I thought was really very petty. Looking back, I feel we were more influential in that session. Obviously, when you stop a budget you think – wow! But I don't think it did a lot of good for our profile. We were only really important when we could materially affect the result of a vote, and that didn't happen all that often.

ALEX NEIL, Scottish National Party MSP

It was challenging, because we had 47 seats, Labour had 46, the Tories and Lib Dems were both on 16, the Greens had two and there was Margo MacDonald. When it came to the crunch, Margo would usually work with us and support us, because her priority was trying to achieve independence, provided of course there was a quid pro quo for Edinburgh. She was a tough negotiator. We all recognised that the chances of the SNP minority government lasting four years were probably quite slim. We thought there would be a honeymoon period, and then they would go for us. I think Alex Salmond was masterly in how he handled that. A very critical role was played by Bruce Crawford, who was the Minister for Parliament. Bruce and Alex together were a formidable team in managing the parliamentary agenda. We were able to carry out manifesto commitments just by shifting alliances on different subjects in different parts of the chamber. So, despite some efforts, the other parties were never quite able to unite enough against us to bring down the government.

JOHN SWINNEY, Scottish National Party MSP, Deputy First Minister and Former Scottish National Party Leader

On the Saturday night after the election, Alex Salmond phoned me and told me that there was no deal with the Liberals, they wouldn't do it, 'Tavish says no'. So, he told me that we were going to form a minority government. I wondered how on earth that was going to work. Our first worry was if we could actually get there, we had to try to get as many votes for Alex Salmond to be First Minister as we could. We managed to do a deal with the Greens, which got us up to 49 votes, which gave as a little bit more distance from the Labour Party. So, we got Alex into office.

But we worried that while Alex might get in, we might not manage to get our Ministers appointed. Because the other parties might gang up on us again. Alex wanted to strike while the iron was hot, so I got involved in all of these convoluted arrangements of how we could choreograph this. Because Alex could not move to appoint his ministers until he had taken the oath as First Minister, and he could not take the oath until he had a parchment signed by Her Majesty the Queen. So, a civil servant left here the night that Alex was appointed, flew to London, and thankfully the Queen had done the very decent thing of waiting up late to sign the document. The civil servant then went on to Euston station and got the sleeper train back to Scotland, arriving here in the morning. Alex went to the court, took the oath, and then came down to the Parliament to appoint the rest of us. Such was our level of worry that we wouldn't be able to get the government up and running.

Once we had it up and running, we had a team of ministers asking, 'Do you think we will last until the summer?' Our whole strategy was to last until the summer. Because we thought if we could last until the summer then we would have a bit of breathing space and could plough on. Of course, we got to the summer, and the next question was if we could get our budget through. That was the next big test. I will never, ever forget the night we got our first budget through. Because that changed the landscape completely. Getting a budget through was the critical thing. The budget allows you to act, you can spend money. A government can face all sorts of parliamentary defeats, provided it isn't on a no confidence motion, you can just shrug your shoulders. We got a fabulous piece of advice from a civil servant, 'You need to demonstrate to Parliament that you can lose and come back the next day'. We brought an issue before the Parliament that we knew we would lose on, that was the cancellation of the Edinburgh trams. We lost, but we came back the next day with new votes that we knew we would win. That got Parliament accustomed to the fact that the government could lose votes but stay in office.

The 2011 Election – Triumph and Disaster

The 2011 election was the most decisive and surprising in the history of the Scottish Parliament. By winning an absolute majority, the SNP paved the way for an independence referendum and marked the start of a new chapter in the Parliament's history in which constitutional politics would be even more prominent. A victory on this scale had been completely unexpected. The Parliament's electoral system meant that a very high level of popular support was necessary to secure a majority, requiring a larger share of the vote than any party had won in a UK general election for a generation. Yet, up until the month before the election, the SNP had been trailing Labour in the polls, looking more likely to lose power than to storm to majority government. While all parties struggled in the face of the SNP's surge, the worst effected were Labour and the Liberal Democrats. While Labour were naturally disappointed to fall short of their expectation of returning to government, their vote share only fell modestly while the loss of seven of their 44 seats was far from an unmitigated disaster.

These outward results hid the extent of the damage to the parliamentary party. The core of the Labour group going into the election had been held together since the early days of the Parliament. However, as it lost 20 of its 35 constituency seats, and gained 13 seats on the list, many of the Labour's experienced members lost their places in the Parliament while a cohort of younger MSPs, many not expecting to be elected and short on experience, joined the group. For the Liberal Democrats, the defeat was more severe. Having been a major force in the Scottish Parliament through its first three sessions, the party saw its public support drop sharply after entering into a coalition government with the Conservatives in Westminster. As a result, the Liberal Democrats saw their representation in the Scottish Parliament crash from 16 seats before the vote to five after, reducing it to a peripheral force.

Members from these three parties discuss the outcome of the election. The SNP's John Mason notes how many within his own party were not expecting the level of success they achieved, with his own victory in overturning a large Labour majority in Glasgow Shettleston coming as a surprise. Johann Lamont of the Labour Party and Mike Rumbles of the Liberal Democrats reflect on the losses suffered by their own parties, in an election in which she narrowly retained her seat and he lost his.

JOHN MASON, Scottish National Party MSP

In 2011, there were a lot of people who were not expected, and did not expect to be elected – and I include myself in that. A host of us weren't expected to be elected, one way you could tell was by looking at which constituencies Alex Salmond was visiting. He hadn't stopped in Glasgow Shettleston, where I was standing. Just before the election, the party started to realise that things were going quite positively. Suddenly, the day before the election, Salmond came to Shettleston. I knew that was the sign that things were turning in our favour. But the final result was still a surprise for a lot of us. There was a lot of euphoria. We had done so well, and we had got a majority. That wasn't meant to happen, the Parliament was designed so that it wouldn't happen, but it did.

JOHANN LAMONT, Labour Party MSP and Former Scottish Labour Leader

The 2011 election was horrible. We lost good colleagues and good friends in 2007, but 2011 was the worst as we had no idea of the scale of it. We didn't see it coming. I've said this publicly before, it's a very personal thing, that sense of losing people, the sense of fear, and knowing that you somehow survived. I remember going to the count and my council colleagues saying, 'It's fine, it's fine.' Then as we watched the boxes stacking up, I saw my majority getting narrower and narrower. We were beginning to hear stories come in from different places of what was going on. I thought I might lose my seat. Before that night I had thought that I had done enough to survive. I remember Charlie Gordon saying, 'It is really tough but I think it's going to be okay for me in Cathcart. We've looked at the figures and I think it's okay.' No. He was away. I did a bit of television work in the BBC studio, and somebody said, 'It looks as if Andy Kerr's gone.' We could see the SNP's Linda Fabiani and her colleagues were jumping up and down, I kept calm and replied, 'We can't be sure, we need to wait for the result.' But I knew that if Linda Fabiani was jumping up and down, then he had lost. We were in denial. But the defeats just came and came.

It's hard to separate the political from the personal, but that sense of rejection was very strong. When we met as a Labour group afterwards, we had this ambivalence. It was our leader Iain Gray who spoke very powerfully about it, saying that there was a number of people coming in off the list because we had done so badly, people who weren't expecting to be elected. We had to tell them, 'You're entitled to enjoy this. This is your opportunity'. But at the same time, we were grieving. We had high hopes of how we were going to do, but we had a very bad campaign and lost so many colleagues.

MIKE RUMBLES, Liberal Democrat MSP

I didn't see the 2011 election result coming until the final week. I had won my seat in 1999, increased my majority in 2003 and increased it again in 2007. I thought I had done a reasonably good job as an MSP, seen thousands of constituents. I thought I was in a good position.

It was in that final week before the election that it clicked that something was wrong. I was out canvassing and a woman came running out, threw her arms around me and said, 'Mike! Look at this house you got me!' I hadn't gotten her the house, I had just written to the council to make sure they had all her correct details. But she thought I had been instrumental in getting her this house. My assistant was ready to put her down as a Lib Dem vote when I asked her if I could rely upon her support. She responded, 'But Mike, I'm voting SNP.' There was a complete disconnection between what you think you do to help people as an MSP, and how they will vote on election day. I just got the impression in the last week of the campaign that things weren't going well. I could tell it was going to go the SNP's way. Just by being out knocking on doors you get a feeling of what's going on. People you might have expected to support you weren't. So, I wasn't surprised at the count. I was hugely disappointed. We had gone from 16 MSPs to five. It was a disaster for the party.

PART 3

The End of Consensus

2011–2018

Budgetary Restraint

Through the first decade of the Parliament's life, the institution benefited from a wider political climate across the United Kingdom in which public sector budgets were generally rising. The 2008 financial crash, and the reduction in public spending that followed it, brought this period to an end. From 2011 and 2012, the SPCB began to reduce its spending sharply, and maintained tight budgetary discipline for years. Staff were called upon to do 'more with less', a dictum that many in the public sector became familiar with in these years. With some areas of the Parliament's business protected, the axe fell more heavily on others. Across the board, there were freezes on pay and a halt on investments. This restraint has had a major impact on the institution. In the short term, there were undoubtedly negative consequences for morale, as individuals feared for their futures and those who remained were stretched more thinly than in the past. In the longer term, the absence of investment has prevented the Parliament from remaining at the cutting edge.

Willie Heigh describes his involvement in implementing some of these cutbacks, while Murdo MacLeod points to the effect they had on his own office.

WILLIE HEIGH, SPCB Head of Project and Programme Management

I was involved directly in two different reviews of budgets in the Parliament. The goal was not to reduce service or to change service, especially for members. That meant there was a lot of cutting back on projects and investments. There wasn't much money for developing things or rolling out new kit. I think the organisation structured itself back as far as it could go. It is never pleasant. I think about 50 people left the organisation at that point, some of them who had been here for quite a while, maybe even from the start. A lot of experience went at that time. I have been involved in a lot of projects in my time here, but working on a project that is set to cut budgets and reduce posts in an office is probably the worst thing I have ever been involved in. You are sitting there with a room full of people and are saying, 'At the moment there are 40 people working in this office. By the end of this review there are going to be 35 people working in this office'. There were guarantees about no compulsory redundancies, but the uncertainty that that causes in an area was not good to see. The more member-facing areas, because of the nature of their work, I think did not take quite so big a hit. They still changed. There were still reductions going on, but compared to some of the other areas, the more back office areas took a proportionally bigger hit in terms of staff and budgets. I think the atmosphere wasn't as bad as it might have been, because we knew that lots of organisations were going through the same thing or worse at that time. We managed it. After a bumpy couple of years when morale was hit, I would say we bounced back quite quickly. Morale is quite good now.

MURDO MACLEOD, SPCB Official Report Sub-Editor

The budget cuts affected our office in the Official Report. Some people took voluntary redundancy. Since then, we have been effectively operating below capacity. It has been very difficult at times, it made a big difference. Parliament got in early in finding efficiencies and finding savings, which I think was a good move because it meant that when swinging cuts were being made elsewhere in the public sector, Parliament could say, 'We got there ahead of you, we've already made savings'. I know a lot of people didn't like it. You don't like having to do more for less. That is effectively the situation that everybody in the public sector was in. It has affected things like technological development especially strongly. The money simply isn't there to do everything that you want to do. There are things you could do with the most up to date technology, which can't be done because the money is not there. We have perhaps fallen behind in some areas as a result. The money will be there at some point in the future, it was there early on. That was a sort of golden period for the public sector when it was able to spend money, because the money was there.

The Independence Referendum and Political Polarisation

Female Presiding Officer

While the Scottish Parliament's record of women's representation within the chamber has been comparatively strong from its foundation, its most senior positions were dominated by men through its first decade. None of its parties were led by women until Wendy Alexander and Annabel Goldie became the Labour and Conservative leaders respectively in 2007, while each of its first three Presiding Officers, and four First Ministers, were men. Tricia Marwick's election as Presiding Officer in 2011 was an important step in this process, which has subsequently seen a woman elected as First Minister and, at one point, all three of the Parliament's largest parties came under female leadership at the same time. Her comments on her gender-related anxieties about taking on this role reflect the concerns of many women who have taken on senior positions that had previously been occupied almost exclusively by men both within the Parliament and beyond during the same period.

TRICIA MARWICK, Former Presiding Officer and Scottish National Party MSP

I was very aware that I was the first female to be a Presiding Officer. I was absolutely terrified, because we have a predominantly male press. I thought that the worst thing that I could have was for any focus to be put on my clothes. For the first while, I always wore dark business suits in the Parliament. I didn't want anybody talking about what colours I was wearing. I was very careful about what colours I did wear when I started to wear them. I couldn't wear yellow in case people thought it was SNP, I couldn't wear red, I couldn't wear blue, I couldn't wear green. I used to worry about this a lot. I generally settled for the Parliament's purple, which is politically neutral. These are things that men don't have to worry about. Luckily, you now see Deputy Presiding Officers, two women at the moment, who don't care about that. I think it would have been an issue right at the beginning, if there were comments on clothes. That was the last thing I needed. But politics and the media have come a long way, even since 2011.

Majority Government

The parliamentary majority the SNP won in 2011 is the only administration of its type that the Scottish Parliament has ever seen. In all other sessions, the cooperation of at least two parties, in one form or another, has been necessary for the institution to function. Although the SNP had technically lost their absolute majority by September 2014, with one member leaving the party to become Presiding Officer, another being suspended from it, and three resigning the whip to become Independents, the SNP retained effective one-party domination throughout the session. This inevitably changed the way in which it governed, and encouraged the development of a more confrontational political atmosphere within the Parliament. Opposition groups were left without any real stake in or influence over government policy, and had no recourse to hold back the SNP from the push towards an independence referendum that most of them opposed.

John Swinney, a key figure in the SNP leadership, and John Mason, one of the party's backbenchers, both recall an initial hope on the part of their party for the collaborative spirit of the previous session to continue, and the failure of that ambition to survive the realities of majority government. Murdo Fraser observes the breakdown of that vision from the viewpoint of the Conservative Party, that shifted from a healthy relationship with the government before 2011, to intense opposition by the end of the session.

JOHN SWINNEY, Scottish National Party MSP, Deputy First Minister and Former Scottish National Party Leader

The Parliament was designed for a situation in which there was no majority. When we won our majority in 2011 we tried to maintain the ethos of securing common ground that we had built up between 2007 and 2011. That became more difficult for two reasons. Firstly, with our majority all the other parties knew that we didn't need them to pass anything. Secondly, we were moving towards the independence referendum and the Parliament was starting to polarise. There was much less of a spirit of collaboration than there was before. A lot of that level of hostility and antagonism was created by the fact that some people in the Parliament wanted independence and some didn't.

JOHN MASON, Scottish National Party MSP

I think in practice that the majority we won in 2011 meant that the SNP could win votes and force through legislation without really consulting anyone. That varied, because many of them had worked with people and consulted with them between 2007 and 2011. So, there was a feeling that both Alex Salmond and Nicola Sturgeon, both leaders, wanted to continue that. But it certainly changed, the arithmetic meant that we didn't need the other parties. I do think that this Parliament works best when one party doesn't have a majority.

MURDO FRASER, Conservative & Unionist Party MSP

There was a change of course in 2011 after the SNP were elected with a majority. The whole approach changed. On the one hand, by that stage we had a Conservative–Liberal Democrat coalition in Westminster that the SNP wanted to position themselves as being in opposition to. In addition, they were determined to push for a referendum on independence, which we were completely against. That meant that what was previously quite a positive relationship between the SNP and the Conservatives came to an end. We ended up being much more oppositional, and the whole focus of the period moved towards the independence referendum.

The 2014 Independence Referendum

The independence referendum was undoubtedly an extraordinary moment in Scottish history. It attracted a higher turnout than any vote, on any issues, anywhere in the United Kingdom since the advent of universal suffrage. Its 85 per cent turnout compared to 64 per cent in the 2010 Westminster election that preceded it, and just 50 per cent in the 2011 Holyrood contest. It sparked a degree of intensity from both sides of the debate that hadn't been seen in Scottish politics in living memory. It also made Scotland the focal point of an international news story, as onlookers from around the world were transfixed by the question of which way the nation's voters would swing.

The campaigning and politics of the referendum were largely the domain of the world outside of the Scottish Parliament rather than the institution itself. Nonetheless, the Parliament was deeply affected by it. Ken Hughes points out that in the event of a 'Yes' vote in favour of independence, the Scottish Parliament would have been transformed from a devolved legislature into the seat of power of a nation state within a very short period of time. As such, the Parliament had to make contingency plans on how it would assume the new power, authority and stature this change would have entailed. The global interest in the referendum drew media from around the world, many of whom chose to use the Parliament as a backdrop to illustrate the debate going on across the country. Ruth Connelly recalls the steps the Parliament took to accommodate this influx. The referendum also affected the day-to-day running of the Parliament. Stephen Imrie points to the palpable increase in political tension, and the dominance of the independence question over all other issues. Finally, the Conservative MSP Murdo Fraser, a fierce defender of the Union, makes a broader comment on the impact the referendum had on the Parliament, both in its short term effect on parliamentary business and political atmosphere and the longer term stature of the institution.

KEN HUGHES, SPCB Assistant Chief Executive

After the SNP got their majority in 2011, it seemed inevitable that there would be an independence referendum. From 2012, I got involved in constitutional work, which involved trying to make sure that the Parliament was best placed and had the capacity to deal with anything put before it. You can't do that after it has already happened, because it takes time to recruit staff, train them and set up lines of enquiry. You have got to anticipate. It is the art of trying to speculate about the possibilities of what could happen and what it would mean for the Parliament in performing its duties. We had plans ready for whichever way that the people of Scotland voted. The biggest challenge was going to be if there was a 'Yes'. Because, for political reasons, it was clear that in the event of a 'Yes' vote we would have not much more than 18 months to start operating as an independent country. The challenge for me was to really think about what the demands and challenges that would have placed upon the Parliament. What I hadn't planned for was for the Prime Minister David Cameron to come out on the morning after the referendum with a commission on further devolution chaired by Lord Smith. Perhaps understandably, we hadn't been fed into any of the thinking on that beforehand. By half past eight that morning, Paul Grice was on the phone to the UK government asking how the Parliament was going to be involved.

In the end, we seconded some people from the Parliament to support the commission to make sure that parliamentary interests were looked after.

RUTH CONNELLY, SPCB Head of Broadcasting

Dealing with the independence referendum was a highlight of my time here. I started getting phone calls about a year before the referendum from Russia, America, Japan, asking to come here. It was dawning on me that this was far larger than the UK and far larger than Europe. It was major. So, I suggested that we needed some sort of facility, a media village. We accredited 853 media people to come here, we needed a big team of volunteers to handle it. We created an information centre where every journalist or media person would arrive, be signed in, collect a badge and be able to ask questions. That was manned virtually 24 hours, and security worked through the night, because people were filming at every hour of the day to broadcast to time zones around the world. The Parliament was being seen globally, from Fiji, to Japan, the Faroe Islands sent somebody, to Iceland, America, Canada, Brazil. Anywhere you could name. It was a massive piece of work, but it was hugely fulfilling to be involved with.

MURDO FRASER, Conservative & Unionist Party MSP

The referendum had both positive and negative impacts on the Parliament. There was a sense that you were dealing with what were really significant issues about Scotland's future, perhaps in a way that the Parliament hadn't really dealt with in the past. The independence question was something that was really significant. Not only in Scottish terms, but in UK and even international terms. I was chair of the Economy Committee at the time, and we did an inquiry which lasted nine months into Scotland's economic future. Every week we were having witnesses around the independence question, and a lot of committees were doing similar work. Independence was scrutinised and debated in great detail. The Parliament really grew up at that point, and became a real focus for national debate.

But there were at least two negatives that I can think of. The first negative was that this meant that a lot of other important business was inevitably squeezed out. There was less time to focus on the health service, or education, or justice, or anything else. That became less important, and less attention was paid to it. The second issue was that politics became much more tribal in a way we hadn't seen in the Scottish Parliament before. The atmosphere in Parliament entered the most heated period I can remember. Debates became much more passionate, and the rhetoric over the independence question grew ever stronger. If you were in the SNP or the Greens you were pro-independence and on one side of the great divide, while the Conservatives, Labour and Liberal Democrats were on the other side of the great divide. I suppose we started working much more closely with Labour and the Lib Dems due to our shared opposition to independence. But it became a much more tribal atmosphere, at times actually quite aggressive and poisonous. Passions were running high. It mattered hugely to people who had been Nationalists all their lives and this was their once in a lifetime opportunity, as well as to those of us who were Unionists and wanted to preserve the United Kingdom. I got very passionate, and that wasn't always a positive experience.

The Persistence of Cooperation

While the polarisation of politics in the Scottish Parliament during the 2010s was very real, it was not absolute. The Parliament continued to function, politicians of different parties still interacted and collaborated on important issues, and they still shared many of the same values and ambitions for Scotland. This reality is obscured from the eyes of the public, with the tightest cooperation often taking place away from their gaze. Jackson Carlaw highlights this side of politics, illustrating that even at its most divided, the Parliament has never become a completely hostile battleground.

JACKSON CARLAW, Conservative & Unionist Party MSP

Partisanship is an obvious thing. I think it's most prevalent in the weakest politicians because I think the bigger politicians, who always have to have a slightly ruthless partisan streak, understand that we work on a much broader canvas than that. I find it fascinating how much progress can be made across party lines on an issue when it isn't in the public spotlight. I know many times I've watched progress being made, and then the public spotlight falls on an issue and all the parties run to the four corners of the boxing ring and tee up for a fight. It is interesting to me that although there is a circus and a theatre to politics, which is very often the bit that is covered, because it's entertaining and the media dwell on it, there's actually a business of politics that goes on in the Parliament across a lot of issues where there is far more cooperation than people would imagine. If you look at the Social Security Bill that was approved unanimously last week by the Parliament, something people imagined would probably rent asunder any consensus between Conservatives, Socialists and Nationalists. Actually, we ended up with an agreement, a Bill that we could all agree to. Or you could look at the work I've been involved in with Alex Neil and Neil Findlay on the transvaginal mesh scandal, where three politicians, three male politicians, from three completely different parties have worked very closely together on a woman's issue. That co-operation exists very often. But I find the lazy partisanship in some of the debates excruciatingly dull.

The Extension of Devolution

For the first decade of the Scottish Parliament's life, the country's devolution settlement remained stable. This began to change after the SNP's ascension to government in 2007. Within months of assuming office, the new administration had taken the symbolic step of retitling the Scottish Executive as the Scottish Government and reopened the constitutional debate that had been relatively muted since 1999 through its forthright advocacy in favour of a referendum on independence. In response to the changing circumstances, the three Unionist parties, Labour, the Conservatives and the Liberal Democrats, joined together to support the creation of the Calman Commission, tasked with investigating ways in which devolution could be strengthened within the United Kingdom. After the Commission published reports in 2008 and 2009, its recommendations formed the basis of the 2012 Scotland Act that transferred new powers to the Scottish Parliament. However, this first round of constitutional change was very quickly overtaken by events. During the 2014 independence referendum, the leaders of the main Unionist parties joined together to promise a stronger Scottish Parliament in the event of a 'No' vote. In order to make good on these assurances, the Prime Minister David Cameron announced the creation of the Smith Commission on the morning after the vote. The Commission acted quickly, publishing its recommendations in 2015, which in turn inspired a further transfer of powers in the 2016 Scotland Act. In a short few years, the Parliament had assumed significant new powers, especially in areas of taxation and welfare. This created a degree of discomfort for the institution, as it attempted to ready itself to make use of its new responsibilities without an accompanying increase in its resources or the expertise of its staff and politicians. The authority of the Parliament is expected to change once again in the coming years. As the United Kingdom completes its exit from the European Union, it is likely that the powers of the Parliament will be altered yet again. However, the precise shape of this future constitutional settlement, and its consequences for the Parliament, remain unclear.

The SPCB staff member Shona Skakle and the senior MSP Linda Fabiani observe some of the issues that have arisen for the Parliament as it has assumed the responsibilities passed on to it in these years, and the ways it has sought to adjust itself.

SHONA SKAKLE, SPCB Head of Enquiries

One of the most significant impacts on us at the information service desk has been the changing legislation in 2012 and 2016 when the Scotland Act was extended, which has brought new powers to the Parliament. In 1999, there were things where part of a topic was the responsibility of the Scottish Parliament, and part was with Westminster. But it was fairly clear where the divisions were. But now with things like social security and income tax, there are some devolved power and a lot that is still reserved. That makes things a bit more complicated, and more complicated for us because we are answering questions on issues where the dividing lines are a lot more grey than they used to be. But it also makes things difficult for members, because they have to get up to speed on these new topics. Part of our job is to support them on that. So that kind of legislative change has a big impact on us.

LINDA FABIANI, Scottish National Party MSP

My concern is that as the Parliament has grown in terms of additional powers, it piles more and more work on the committees, more and more work on individual members. There are people who are on three committees, and that is hard work. There was a period when I was in the Corporate Body, which is like a committee, I was on another committee as a full member then I was chairing a separate committee. Hard work. The idea of colleagues, especially those who have only come in recently, being thrown onto that many committees, with all the work involved, is problematic. It's something that we have to look at, because you get the complaints about members not being able to do proper pre-legislative scrutiny, let alone impose legislative scrutiny, which is something that we all think is important. The time constraints are just ridiculous. With the increases in the Parliament's powers in recent years, we have tax powers, we have welfare powers. There's an awful lot of additional stuff that committees have to deal with. I think this is a problem for everybody. The amount of legislation that's going through this Parliament is huge. We were set up for the original Scotland Bill. We have maintained the same number of people and the same number of staff, but given them extra work. There are huge pressures. Everyone has more and more work to do all the time with each additional piece of devolution.

Outside Organisations and the Parliament

The Scottish Parliament is very proud of the level of interaction it maintains with outside organisations, particularly NGOs. These groups are invariably consulted on legislation passing through the Parliament, invited to express their views, give evidence or provide advice. This has given them a real influence over the policies the Parliament puts forward. The extent of this involvement has had an effect on how politics is practised in Holyrood. Jackie Baillie observes that during the SNP's majority administration, in the absence of a route to changing government policy through debate in the chamber, these outside organisations became the most effective bodies in influencing the government. This power is not evenly distributed among different interests. As Tavish Scott makes clear, the better organised and more energetic lobbies have been able to gain a disproportionately loud voice in the political process.

JACKIE BAILLIE, Labour Party MSP

The SNP didn't need to talk to anybody between 2011 and 2016. Not to us, or the Liberals, or the Tories. What I learned was that the only way you get a change was if civic Scotland didn't like what was going on. So, a lot of our time in the Labour Party was spent engaging with people outside of Parliament, as they were the ones bringing change to the Parliament. The majority government didn't need to pay attention to us in opposition, but it would pay attention to civic Scotland. That became an opportunity for us to look outward rather than inwards, so that was no bad thing. In the beginning with the foundation of the Parliament, civic Scotland had a hand in shaping the Parliament through their participation in the Constitutional Convention. Since then, as expert witnesses to committees and lobbyists for their own sectors, they have been pretty effective.

When there has been a majority government, they have helped the Parliament by acting as a check on the government. In a minority there is no monopoly on good ideas, and a lot of them come from the third sector. When a government can say, 'We have gotten the backing of Shelter or Crisis for our homeless strategy' it is quite powerful for the rest of the Parliament.

TAVISH SCOTT, Liberal Democrat MSP and Former Scottish Liberal Democrat Leader

Business and industry has been pretty hopeless at getting in here and trying to argue for change. They only turn up once a year when the budget comes out, and that's usually only to talk about business rates. NGOs and the voluntary sector, and quite a lot of other organisations, have been very adept and clever about looking into how to influence the Parliament. Business has been strikingly bad at it. We all extol the virtues of a sustainable growing economy, but the business men and women who are key to achieving that, with some wonderful exceptions, have been particularly bad at lobbying. I had thought they would end up being the most professional lobby we would face. But actually, some of the environmental and animal welfare organisations have been far better at it. If you don't shout, people don't notice you.

Donald Trump Comes to Holyrood

The Scottish Parliament has attracted an array of high profile visitors over the years, ranging from the Dalai Lama to Bob Geldof. Yet perhaps the most memorable, and certainly the most colourful, visitor was the future President of the United States Donald Trump, who came to the Parliament to speak before one of its committees in 2012. Trump had been a highly vocal critic of the Scottish Government's renewable energy strategy, that involved encouraging largescale investment in wind energy. In particular, he was irked by plans to build a windfarm within sight of one of his golf courses on the Menie estate in Aberdeenshire, which he claimed would be an eyesore in an otherwise beautiful landscape. When a Scottish Parliament committee began investigating the impact of renewable energy, Trump was invited to give evidence before the committee. To the surprise of some, the billionaire tycoon accepted. The visit of one of the world's most recognisable figures to the Parliament drew in a great deal of excitement, media attention and boisterous protestors.

One of the organisers of the visit, Stephen Imrie, speaks about how the process of bringing Donald Trump to Holyrood was managed, while journalist Colin Mackay shares two of his favourite anecdotes from the day itself.

STEPHEN IMRIE, SPCB Clerk to the Justice Committee

I was the person responsible for organising the visit of Donald Trump to the Parliament. It was a crazy day, in terms of interest and the media and people outside and all that kind of stuff. But the fact that we organised it well meant that it passed off smoothly and professionally. Which is what you try to achieve as a parliamentary official. Little did I know when I was stood behind that man, I could have whispered over and said, 'Do you think you'll ever be President of the United States one day?'

I was the clerk of the Economy Committee and working with Murdo Fraser, who was the Convener. We were doing an inquiry into renewable energy and Donald Trump, now President Trump, was quite antagonistic towards a wind farm off the coast of Aberdeenshire near one his golf courses. It started with a kind of joking comment, 'Do you think he'll ever come', and we all kind of laughed and then someone said, 'Why don't we just try?' So, I was left with the task of going off and trying to find how to contact Donald Trump and get him to come along. Amazingly, he did.

Then I had the opportunity, because I was looking after him, of meeting him and his staff in a waiting room while we were waiting for the committee meeting to start. He didn't say very much, he was quite quiet. I think he was just thinking about what he was going to say at the committee meeting and preparing himself. His staff seemed quite relaxed. It really was an amazing afternoon, I've never seen a committee room so busy with people, I had to put extra seats in. Then we did a press conference afterwards, and my abiding memory of that was taking him from this waiting room into the committee room. I was the person that opened the door between the waiting room and the committee room, and as I opened the door for him to walk in the cameras just went off, the flash bulbs, and I've never felt anything like it. It was like walking down the red carpet at the Oscars ceremony or something like that.

But he had a good press conference, it went off well. Afterwards, he and his team said that they lived in a crazy media bubble, but they never experienced anything quite like their visit to the Parliament, and they were appreciative of how well it was managed. It was up to the members to ask questions about wind farms, it was my job to make sure the events were organised well and safely and that Parliament's reputation was upheld. Although it was a bit of a media circus, we were there to ask serious questions about his views on renewable energy and wind farms and why he was against them when others in Scotland were supportive.

COLIN MACKAY, Holyrood Editor for *STV News*

When Donald Trump came to give evidence at the Scottish Parliament committee about the planning application for the wind farm off the coast of his Aberdeenshire golf course, there were two great moments. There was an activist who had the most fantastic protest against Trump. He carried a balloon around with him all day and he tried to get behind Trump. He rubbed the balloon up against his jumper and then held it above Trump's head. That made his hair stand on end. It was one of the most original political protests I'd ever seen.

Trump had his security guards with him that day, and he had a big guy who used to work as a New York cop. He was a really imposing guy, really impressive. One of the young police officers down in the Parliament noticed that this security guy had a big bulge under his jacket. He thought that it was a gun, and he was going to have to lift him. So the policeman said, 'Excuse me sir, what is that under your jacket?' Trump's security guy just pulled back his jacket to show an enormous can of Elnett hairspray. Then a little while later, the same policeman was outside the committee room in the Parliament, and Trump was in this little anteroom where witnesses go while they wait, and as the policeman was going past he could hear a, 'Shhh, shhh' noise, as he was getting his hair done perfectly before coming into the committee.

The Youngest MSP

The archetypal elected politician is securely middle-aged. Immediately after the 2016 election, the average age of the Scottish Parliament's MSPs was 49. Following the 2017 general election, the average age of MPs in the House of Commons was 50. Most members do not reach Parliament until their 30s, forties, or even later. A small minority have been elected in their mid- to late-20s, with only a handful of younger individuals having stepped foot in any Parliament in the British Isles. This is typical of legislatures around the world. In this, the Green Party's Ross Greer stands out as an exception. Twenty-one years old at the time of his election in 2016, just less than four years older than devolution itself, he was, and remains, by far the youngest individual ever to serve in the Scottish Parliament. Most of his colleagues were twice his age or more. Only the election of Mhairi Black to the House of Commons at the age of 20 in 2015, breaking centuries old records, obscures how unusual this situation is. Greer takes the opportunity to detail his experience as the Parliament's youngest MSP.

ROSS GREER, Scottish Green Party MSP

I am probably the first MSP who can't remember a time before the Scottish Parliament. My perspective is different, devolution has been the norm my entire living memory. I can't conceive of a time before there was a Scottish Parliament. Scotland having a different relationship with the rest of the UK is just not something I have a lived experience of. For me, it's a matter of history, it's something that I studied rather than something I experienced. That probably gives me a different perspective on the Parliament itself and its permanence. For those who can remember a time before devolution, it probably feels a little bit less permanent. For me, it is utterly inconceivable that there will ever not be a Scottish Parliament, because as far as I'm concerned, there has never not been one.

I have been very conscious of my age at times. I think that there are quite a number in the Parliament who weren't quite sure at first about how the relationship between us would play out. In many cases, I'm the same age as folks' kids, in plenty of cases I'm the same age as folks' grandchildren. Christine Grahame, the Deputy Presiding Officer, was telling me just how much it distresses her that I am the same age as her grandchildren. It was funny, and reminded me that it must be quite an awkward experience for a lot of people. There are plenty of folks in here now who are my age who work for MSPs or who work in the building in another capacity, and often in more junior roles, because at my age most people are just starting their career. I was absolutely the other end of the spectrum in that hierarchy. There have been plenty of occasions where, for example, I am on a visit with other MSPs and the presumption from the people we are visiting is that I am the assistant, just because people make assumptions around age. The young man must always be there to support the older people. You see people take a step back and realise it's actually the other way around. But in this building and from parliamentary staff, on the other hand, I genuinely feel that I have been treated on par with everyone else.

Another concern I had was that there was a threat from some people in the media to depoliticise me. That it would be easier to deal with Ross Greer the youngest MSP, rather than Ross Greer the Green MSP for the West of Scotland. I was elected to be the Green MSP for the West of Scotland, not to be the youngest MSP. However, overwhelmingly I have been allowed to do my job as a Green MSP for my region, and I think that is a credit to my colleagues across all parties who have treated me with respect and as a serious political opponent. Being an MSP is a hard job, and it should be a hard job, but I have had an experience that I hope other young people can too. I have no intention of holding on to the record, I don't want to be Scotland's youngest MSP forever. We allow 16- and 17-year-olds to vote. There is absolutely no reason why there shouldn't be a younger MSP in the future.

The Contemporary Parliament

Continuous Campaigning

Through the 2010s, Scotland faced an unusually larger number of nationwide electoral contests, some of which were among the most intense in its history. Scotland's electoral calendar had become more crowded with the advent of devolution, that meant that the country's voters had to regularly elect the members of two separate parliaments rather than one. The situation was further exacerbated by a significant increase in the use of referendums during this decade, with plebiscites of this kind having been used in only a handful of occasions in Scottish and British political history prior to the 2010s. After the 2010 UK general election, there were Holyrood elections and a referendum on the voting system to be used in British general elections in 2011. While there was then a gap of three years until the next vote, the Edinburgh Agreement of 2012 that set down the terms of the independence referendum ensured that low-level campaigning in Scotland did not stop entirely. In the spring of 2014, Scots voted in the last European elections to involve the United Kingdom before the country's scheduled exit from the European Union, before casting their verdict in the independence referendum. Less than a year, later they voted in the 2015 general election. They then cast their ballots in the 2016 Scottish Parliamentary election, followed shortly by the European Union membership referendum. Respite only arrived after a further UK general election in 2017. This brought to an end a period of almost ceaseless electioneering, that had grown particularly intense in the period between 2014 and 2017.

Fiona Hyslop admits to the stress this election calendar caused for politicians and activists, and the negative consequences it had on the proper functioning of the Parliament.

FIONA HYSLOP, Scottish National Party MSP

We've basically had constant campaigning since probably around 2010. There was either an election or a referendum nearly every year. It hasn't helped us politicians in terms of our aging process. I've always held that I think the constant campaigning does have an impact on individuals. Clearly, because of the levels of effort and focus that you are deploying. Not only are you representing your constituency and your regular parliamentary work, those of us who are government ministers are still doing that, you are also on the campaign trail. I love campaigning, I love knocking on doors, I love talking to people, but that's a lot of effort over sustained period of time. I think it effects parliamentary business. You can always tell when there's an election coming, because the debates become a bit more tribal, a bit more points scoring, and it's not as productive.

2016 *Parliament Induction Process*

After seeing relations between MSPs deteriorate during session four, many in the Parliament were seriously concerned. This sort of partisan animosity was far divorced from the Parliament's founding ideals, made for a much less pleasant working environment and undermined the ability of MSPs to work together effectively. One solution offered to ease these tensions was an induction programme for the MSPs that were newly elected in 2016. This new group was unusually large. With significant numbers of members either choosing not to stand or losing their seats, there were 51 new MSPs after the election, the most since 1999. It was hoped that a joint induction process would encourage social interaction and friendship across parties, spilling over into a happier atmosphere across the Parliament.

Former Presiding Officer Tricia Marwick comments on her regret at the loss of the unified spirit of the Parliament's early days, and her hope that the new induction procedure could begin to recapture it. Journalist Kirsten Campbell then delves more deeply into the impact that the process has had on the Parliament.

TRICIA MARWICK, Former Presiding Officer and Scottish National Party MSP

The 1999 cohort were a much tighter group, we were a lot more collegiate. We managed to make friends across the parties. As time has gone on, there are fewer friendships across the parties. I think that is regrettable. The 1999 group were brought together by the building project and all the bad publicity we got. We realised that we were all in it together. There was a sort of siege mentality that I think bound us together. On top of that, we were the first MSPs. We learnt how to be parliamentarians from each other, and through that learnt to be friends. People haven't had those same shared circumstances in subsequent cohorts of MSPs in 2003, 2007 or 2011.

My very last act as Presiding Officer was to have an induction course for new MSPs, because there had never been a proper course before. We had lunch together with a night time reception for them and their families, where they would all come together. I hoped that by doing this we could try to get across the message that it is okay to have friends throughout the Parliament, even if they are in different parties.

KIRSTEN CAMPBELL, BBC Scotland Political Journalist

The current session is interesting in that it has recaptured some of the friendliness of the first years of the Parliament. The atmosphere has reverted back to where it used to be before the 2011 to 2016 session. I don't think that is necessarily anything to do with going back to a minority government. There was a very big turnover of MSPs in the 2016 election, a lot of new faces. The Parliament introduced a new induction process. All the newbies from the different parties went on courses together to learn how to press their button to vote, how to request to speak, and that kind of thing. They would do all these courses together, it was a bit like starting university. All the people that were in your kitchen or on your floor in halls became your buddies. There's a lot of cross-party friendships in the 2016 intake, just like there were in 1999. I think we've recreated that 1999 atmosphere, and that's partly because of the induction process allowing people from different parties to get to know each other, going through the same experiences at the same time.

The Return to Minority Government

In 2016, the SNP were unable to repeat the feat they had accomplished at the previous election, falling two seats short of winning another majority, with 63 of the Parliament's 129 seats. Nonetheless, they remained in power as a minority government. This brought an end to the SNP's period of almost untrammelled control, paving the way for government defeats. However, this administration was very different to the previous minority government they had controlled in session three. Firstly, they only needed the backing of two opposition MSPs to win majority support in the chamber, meaning there was little need to assemble the broad political coalitions they had pursued in the 2007 to 2011 period. Equally as important, the range of potential political partners had narrowed sharply. In light of the deepening of divisions over the previous five years, Unionist parties found it far more difficult to lend their support to an independence-supporting government than they had in the past. The SNP therefore came to depend upon the collaboration of the only other pro-independence party, the Greens, in the most significant votes.

The Deputy First Minister John Swinney and the Green MSP Ross

Greer describe the way in which the political context and parliamentary arithmetic in place since 2016 has shaped politics.

JOHN SWINNEY, Scottish National Party MSP, Deputy First Minister and Former Scottish National Party Leader

In this session, we have got to more actively seek other partners on certain things that we did when we had a majority. We have to seek agreements with others. That can be enormously challenging, sometimes you don't manage it. The politics are more polarised now than they were during our previous term of minority government, and there isn't much goodwill to try to find common ground as there was in that period. I think that is principally a result of the constitutional debate. But generally, personal relationships in the Parliament are poorer than they were. That effects the whole environment. I also think that there must be frustration in the other parties about the fact that they have not been in government for a long time. We've been in government for 11 years now. The Liberal–Labour Executive only governed for eight years. I think there is a burgeoning sense of resentment that we've won so comprehensively for so long.

ROSS GREER, Scottish Green Party MSP

We are in a unique position in this session, as the government only needs the votes of the Greens to get themselves to a majority in the chamber. They only need the votes of one other party, but in the broader political environment we are the only other party that supports independence. That means that the other three parties will often rule themselves out of even engaging with the government on issues that have nothing to do with independence, on the budget for example. That gives us a huge opportunity, because unless the SNP want the government to fall, they need to negotiate with the Greens to get things through. So, we've gone from a place where the role of a small party in the Parliament was to put issues on the agenda and create pressure, to where we are in a position as a small party to influence and change policy on a regular basis. This is the most influential the Greens have been in the history of devolution so far, because the arithmetic works out so well. There was a session where we had one more MSP than we have now, but there was a coalition government with a parliamentary majority, so the opportunity to influence them were limited. That has required a shift in how we operate as a political party. You can't talk in vague terms on specific policy proposals. The Greens have done plenty of that in the past. We need to come into meetings with prepared and costed proposals on exactly how we would implement X, Y and Z. It's harder, it's more challenging, but it is a colossal opportunity for us.

The Culture of the SNP Group

At the publication of this text in May 2019, the Scottish National Party have been in government for 12 years. Since their blowout success at the 2011 Holyrood elections, they have begun to dominate Scottish politics with a series of heavy election victories in both Scottish and UK-wide contests. In the same period, their elected politicians, particularly those within the Scottish Parliament, have gained a reputation for unity and discipline, with very few members speaking out publicly against the leadership or voting against it. Both these elements are significant departures for a party with a long history of electoral defeats and internal disputes. They have contributed to the development of a new political culture within the SNP's parliamentary group, that is notably different to the party of old.

Linda Fabiani notes that while members of her generation saw election victory as something exceptional, for many younger SNP MSPs it has become routine. John Swinney then compares the united front shown by SNP members since entering government with the more rebellious party he led during the early years of the Parliament, pointing to possible reasons for this shift in attitude.

LINDA FABIANI, Scottish National Party MSP

There is a generation of SNP MSPs who have never known anything else but success. It doesn't matter what discussions you have, or what you try to impart to them about being in opposition, if you haven't experienced it yourself it's very different. There are times when there's almost no recognition from them that things could ever be any different. I think if it did become different, and we lost power, it would be a shock. They are all smart people so they might adapt and they would learn, but they haven't had to go back into opposition yet. It is horrible.

JOHN SWINNEY, Scottish National Party MSP, Deputy First
Minister and former Scottish National Party Leader

When I was the SNP's leader between 2000 and 2004, the overwhelming majority of our members were party stalwarts who were prepared to
work for a common purpose. But there were a number of members who
were individualistic. It was hard to get them to cut it out, and that often
made us look divided. We still have real individuals in our group, but we
now have a culture which is based heavily on self-discipline and mutual
respect. That is a product of the 2007 to 2011 Parliament. We got 47
seats and Labour got 46. I was in charge of the logistics of forming the
government. When Alex Salmond told me that we were forming a minority government, I looked at the lists and wondered how this was going
to work. We had folk in our group who wouldn't toe the party line, it
was never going to work. What I didn't bank on, was that every single
member looked at the situation and realised that if they put a foot wrong
then our government would go down. That created a culture of self-discipline and mutual respect almost overnight. In that Parliament, our whips
hardly had anything to do. Nobody had to be brought into line. People
realised that if you didn't contribute to our internal discussions then the
government would lose, and the party would never forgive them. The iro-
ny was that the difficult electoral arithmetic created a culture within the
SNP that most parties would give their right arm for.

The New Second Party

While the 2016 election did not change the governing party, it did up-
turn some core ideas about Scottish politics. Since the inauguration of
the Scottish Parliament, the Conservatives had become used to their status as the distant third party, at times only narrowly avoiding slipping
behind the Liberal Democrats to become the fourth. At the same time,
although they had been overtaken by the SNP in 2007, Labour held firm
to their status as the Parliament's second party and its main opposition.
Few regarded any other party as presenting a credible alternative to an
SNP-led government. This changed in 2016, as the Conservatives doubled
the size of their parliamentary group to win 31 seats, substantially more
than they had ever had before. As the Tories celebrated, Labour suffered
severe losses, falling to 24 seats. This was just two fifths of the total they

had held at their highpoint in the first Scottish Parliamentary election in 1999. The Conservative Party rose to replace Labour as the second largest in the Parliament and become the main opposition, a turn of events that would have seemed scarcely imaginable when the institution first opened its doors.

The perspectives of both the winners and losers of this transition, and the impacts on their respective parties, are displayed by Murdo Fraser of the Conservative Party and Jackie Baillie of the Labour Party.

MURDO FRASER, Conservative & Unionist Party MSP

Becoming the Parliament's second largest party affected us in a number of ways. The biggest change was psychological. Ever since 1999, we had been the third party. The Parliament, and Scottish politics, was seen as being Labour versus the SNP. But suddenly we had supplanted Labour, we were now the second party and Scottish politics was being refocused as being the SNP versus the Conservatives. For those of us who had been around for a while, it was very refreshing. It was quite a boost to morale to suddenly be in that position. There was also a physical change. In the chamber, we moved to the other side of the aisle, to where Labour had previously been, which was symbolically important to us. From the point of view of working practices, it meant that we had a lot more colleagues to rely on. So, when it came to debates, in the past we might have had two or three people speaking, while now we would have five or six. There were a lot more colleagues in committees, putting forward the Conservative view. It created a sense of there being a team of people around you, backing you up. There were a lot more Conservative voices being heard. We are able to have much more influence on the political debate than we did previously.

JACKIE BAILLIE, Labour Party MSP

The 2016 election was terrible. I'll start with the physical, as that has stuck in my mind. Swapping sides in the chamber with the Conservatives was awful. It gives you a different perspective in the Parliament than we had before. It felt very strange. It was quite extraordinary to see voters who had previously been supporting us suddenly choose to move over to the Conservatives, principally because they were perceived to be stronger on the constitution. I regularly had people come to me on the street, regular Labour supporters, who said they would support me in the constituency vote but they would back the Tories on the list. I watched people move away from us. Our country had become divided on the constitution – you are for or against independence, there was no room in the middle for nuance.

The Changed Fortunes of the Liberal Democrats

For the first 12 years of the Scottish Parliament, the Liberal Democrats were one of its most prominent players. Although the fourth party throughout this period, they maintained a large MSP group and wielded an important influence on government. After serving alongside the Labour Party in coalition between 1999 and 2007, they retained a strong position even after going into opposition as the SNP minority administration sought support from all corners. All this came to an end in 2011. Since then, the party's MSP group has been reduced to five, less than a third of its former strength. From the 2016 election, it has fallen behind the Greens to become the fifth, and smallest, party in the Parliament. It has also found itself pushed further from the power to effect governments. The SNP's majority in session four shut all opposition parties out, but the Liberal Democrats have been unable to exert the level of influence they might otherwise have been able to during the current session, as the constitutional polarisation of Scottish politics has placed substantial barriers against collaboration between Unionist and pro-independence parties. This has left the Liberal Democrats marginalised, and gravely diminished in status within the Scottish Parliament.

Mike Rumbles and Tavish Scott, the two most experienced still-serving Liberal Democrat MSPs, observe the ways in which this decline has transformed the party's position and behaviour within the Parliament.

MIKE RUMBLES, Liberal Democrat MSP

It has changed a lot. We were always very influential during the first two sessions as a part of the coalition government, and I still thought we were influential in the third Parliament until the Tories really got their act together with the SNP. Now it is very different. We almost always vote together, which wasn't the case in the past. There is no real need to rebel, because the small numbers mean we can have a really good discussion to decide what the Liberal Democrat position is going to be. The difference is that we are a much smaller organisation. When we were here before, people were interested in our views. Now, we are the fifth party in Parliament, and the media don't bother after the first three. It's the SNP, the Conservatives, Labour. The Greens and ourselves hardly get a look in. It's part of the media's approach, it's difficult enough to try to get three views, let alone five views on any particular story. So, I understand why we are not covered as much as we would like. Before, the media were always interested. You couldn't walk down the corridor without somebody stopping you and asking for your view. Sometimes that would get you into trouble. It's different now, it's far more difficult to get your views across in the media. The workload has also changed, because now we are responsible for far greater coverage. With only five MSPs, we have to divvy up all of the subjects of 18 or so committees. It's far more difficult to cover that with our numbers. We are also only on, I think, a third of committees. Something like two thirds of them pass us by, we have to make an extra effort to find out what is going on. Whereas in the past we always had people on the committees who could report back to the group. Our task is much more difficult now.

TAVISH SCOTT, Liberal Democrat MSP and Former Scottish Liberal Democrat Leader

Falling behind the Greens in 2016 hasn't really made any difference to the Liberal Democrats. We are still both very small, neither of us have a convenership and both have less choice in terms of committees. The structure of the Parliament at the moment is really hard on the Greens and the Liberal Democrats, because every MSP has to sit on two committees each, and in our case four of the five of us have constituencies as well. There is no space, you can't do it all brilliantly. You have to do the parts that you really enjoy well, and just keep up with the other stuff. You are meant to be scrutinising the government, but there are only so many hours in the day. What comes first? The constituency, then committee work, we also have to make time to speak in the chamber, and so on. Members of small parties are left with a very heavy workload.

Men o Independent Mind

There are many aspects of the Scottish Parliament that have not reached the heights of excellence its founders had hoped for. One of the widest incongruences between their limitless vision and the sober reality has been in the independence, or lack of it, displayed by the bulk of its MSPs. Although an assembly of freethinking talents was perhaps unrealistic for a Parliament that party machines were always likely to dominate, the Scottish Parliament has been even less successful in promoting this sort of atmosphere than Westminster. There have been fewer rebellions against party leaderships in key votes and fewer members willing to go against the grain of mainstream opinion. Party whips have reigned supreme, snuffing out dissent with comparatively little difficulty. This culture has, if anything, grown more stifled over the years.

Members from each of the three largest parties, the Conservative Murdo Fraser, the SNP's Alex Neil and Labour's Jackie Baillie, comment on this aspect of politics in the Scottish Parliament and seek to posit explanations for its development.

MURDO FRASER, Conservative & Unionist Party MSP

One of the biggest disappointments about the Parliament was that when it was set up there was a lot of discussion about moving past Westminster traditions like the party whipping system. We would see individual MSPs have much more freedom of thought, and have the chance to develop their own ideas, free of party-political influence. That never happened here. In fact, I think that the opposite happened. Because the Parliament was smaller, because the party groups were smaller, because in virtually every Parliament there has been a very fine balance between the parties, there has been very little flexibility for individual MSPs to take independent views. You can probably count on the fingers of one hand, or maybe two, the number of times we've had large numbers of MSPs rebelling against their party. At Westminster, you see many more individual MPs from all different parties who are prepared to plough their own furrow and take an independent view. Numbers play a part. At Westminster, there are more than 600 MPs, in the Conservative group alone there are more than 300 people. So even within the Conservative Party at Westminster, there is a broad spectrum of opinions, characters and interests.

There are very ambitious people who want to go for ministerial office, people who are happy to be long-term backbenchers, people who want to develop careers as chairs of select committees. There are people who are always loyal to the party line, and people who are serial rebels who will be the whips' nightmares. It is a much more diverse collection of individuals. The Scottish Parliament has not had the same broad range and diversity of people attracted to it as the original founders of devolution might have hoped for. I don't think that has been a positive thing for the Parliament. I have some sadness that the great flourishing of independent thought that was envisioned never really came about.

ALEX NEIL, Scottish National Party MSP

The smaller size of the chamber gave the party leaderships far too much control over all aspects of the running of the Parliament. I think one of the mistakes David Steel made as Presiding Officer right at the beginning was that he tended to sign up the party leaders on issues like salaries, allowances and so on. Backbenchers were left out in the cold in these discussions. The small size of the Parliament has meant that each party group has been small as well. The largest ever party group was the SNP on 69 members, but that is still a relatively small parliamentary party. The largest Labour group was 56, the Lib Dems at 17, the Tories 31. These are all small groups, so they have a different dynamic. It is very difficult to be a rebel in a small group. So, the party leaders and the party whips have a much tighter grip over their MSPs. We also haven't attracted enough independent-minded people to the Parliament. I don't necessarily mean individuals have to leave their parties and be elected as Independents like Margo MacDonald, but some people who have more backbone and will stand up for what they believe in, instead of kowtowing to party leaderships would benefit us. There are a lot of people who have recently entered the Scottish Parliament without a political hinterland. It has made things duller. There are far too many MSPs, from all parties, who before they speak get a briefing from the central unit, or actually get their speech written for them, and just read it out like nodding donkeys. I think that is bad for the Parliament.

JACKIE BAILLIE, Labour Party MSP

Committees are where probably things have changed most. I remember in the early days there was a health committee where the average age was in the mid-60s. These were people whom the whips could not control. They were our older members, they had been round the block. You had people like Mary Scanlan from the Tories, Ross Finnie from the Lib Dems, Richard Simpson from Labour, Christine Grahame from the SNP and others besides. You would have struggled to work out which party they were, because they hunted as a pack. It was a very impressive committee to be a part of, because they cared about the issues and not about political divisions. Today, as a committee we can take evidence from witnesses, we can see where something is going. But at the end of the day, we will divide on party lines. And that's so disappointing, it's genuinely so disappointing.

It has developed that way because backbenchers need to be loyal to the government. The backbenches in my day used to tear strips off ministers from their own government if they didn't perform appropriately. It just seems to be the culture of, 'If you're a backbencher you need to be a cheerleader for the government', is more prevalent than it was before. When I was on the backbenches, if there was a constituency issue, I would shout about it. And I did, about the Vale of Leven hospital, and poor Malcolm Chisholm got reshuffled after that. I was dreadfully sorry for him, because he's a pal. But my top priority, the only reason I'm elected, is for my constituents. Now there are members who sit there, they have issues in their constituency, but because they are government backbenchers they won't raise them in the chamber. I think they are doing a disservice to their constituents.

The Personal Toll of Politics

There are few occupations that enjoy less sympathy from the public than elected politics. In many quarters, politicians are disdainfully regarded as a distant, manipulative, self-serving and privileged caste separated from people's everyday concerns. Yet, faced with a demanding workload, often hostile scrutiny of their every action and unstable employment that could be terminated at any moment by a swing in the public mood, the stresses they face as individuals are great. Underneath the party labels, they are all regular people who face a very real personal toll from the career path they have chosen. Three aspects of the personal demands politicians in the Scottish Parliament confront are examined below.

Parenthood and the Parliament

Traditionally at Westminster, politics, with its long and unpredictable hours, has been ill suited to parents seeking to raise a family. Just as it did in many other areas, the Scottish Parliament made a conscious effort from the start to be different in this regard, and create a more family-friendly environment. Three members who each raised young children while serving in the Parliament, Ken Macintosh, Fiona Hyslop and Jackie Baillie, discuss their efforts to balance their work and home lives.

KEN MACINTOSH, Presiding Officer and Former Labour Party MSP

My oldest son was born five days before I was elected. I've had another five children since then, six altogether. I got married, became an MSP and had six kids. From the outset, the Parliament itself always aimed to be family friendly. When we came into being 20 years ago, sittings in Westminster didn't start until the middle of the afternoon and they could go on all night. The place was filled with bars. We took a different approach. We aimed to keep nine to five hours, constituency days on Mondays and Fridays were protected, and decision time was set every day at five o'clock. Everything revolves around decision time, which is a very good discipline to have, because it means that our hours are regular and predictable. We try to behave like a normal institution with relatively normal hours. Admittedly, politics isn't normal. You go to meetings in the evenings and weekends, politics doesn't ever stop. But, while politics itself isn't particularly family friendly, the Parliament is. It's been fairly good at providing the anchor of regular, routine, predictable, hours to your life, which has been invaluable for me as a family person. I think I would have struggled to juggle my work and family life if I'd been at Westminster. I am very grateful for the Scottish Parliament's approach, and I'm anxious that it maintains it, in the interests of MSPs, visitors and staff alike.

FIONA HYSLOP, Scottish National Party MSP

I think it has been important that the Parliament has always tried to be as family friendly as it could be. It has been very challenging, and we can't pretend that it is as family friendly as people first thought it would be. I was very fortunate to be a Lothian MSP and then lately Linlithgow's constituency member. That meant I could get home every day. I made a point that on a Monday and a Friday, when Parliament doesn't sit, I would walk my children to school and that would be a time that I would always have with them. They knew that during the week they wouldn't see me very much, but then they had active lives as well.

Of course, I am one of the few people who has also had a baby since becoming elected. When I first got elected I had an 18-month-old and a three-year-old, and then I had my youngest son in July 2004, he was born just as this new Parliament building was being opened. I came in to get my pass, and there were tours going around the Parliament of journalists. This was the first time they had ever seen this new building, but they must have heard the cries of the baby and of course, you know journalists and babies, they flocked over and we ended up taking a photograph of me and my newborn baby in one of the ports in the Parliament. It ended up being in the newspapers the next day, I think it was perhaps symbolic. It was a new start for the building and it was a new start for me, it was a new child. I think the fact that I've been able to bring up three children, one of whom was born during the lifetime of this Parliament, shows that you can have a life, have a family, have children and be a successful women politician and serve your constituency.

JACKIE BAILLIE, Labour Party MSP

Early on, because I had a 7-year-old daughter, I decided that either I put her to bed at night or took her to school in the morning. They couldn't have me at both ends of the day, but they could have me late or early. I remember Frank McAveety, myself and Wendy Alexander were on the same team. Wendy suggested that our first picture should be at Victoria Quay in Edinburgh at seven in the morning. I said, 'Hello! Victoria Quay is in Edinburgh, I've got a child. What are you thinking about?' So, there are moments where you just need to set your boundaries, and then it's all doable. You can have a child and family and pay them attention, but still do your job and do it effectively. You just need to make sure you prioritise what's important.

I want to say that the Parliament is accommodating of the needs of parents, because in theory it absolutely was. But I have watched colleagues in here struggle. There is a crèche, which is great, but your childcare tends to be based closer to home, those are the networks you rely on. So, the crèche is great for the witnesses and visitors to the Parliament, but it's not something you can rely on as a member. There were times when the Parliament would sit late, nothing like as bad as in Westminster, but that disrupted routines. But I think having the core working time as office hours was a correct decision to do. Every organisation suffers from those who want to be present. When someone stays late at night at their desk you think, 'Oh my goodness, they must be very busy'. Not necessary. Women work differently, and we might do it late at night, but we get through it. It is a demanding job, and it has only gotten more so as the years have gone on. But you can do it.

Pressures of Ministerial Office

Ultimately, almost all politicians dream of serving in government as ministers. These roles are the most senior and prestigious in politics, and crucially give members the chance to actively shape policy on a daily basis. Yet these high-ranking positions entail additional challenges. SNP MSP Humza Yousaf, who took on ministerial office just a year after his first election, admits that the demands of his post, and his individual determination to justify his early promotion, put huge personal stress on him.

HUMZA YOUSAF, Scottish National Party MSP

You end up sacrificing a lot personally as a minister. I'm in a much better place now than I used to be. I've got a much better work–life balance, I take weekends, I try to finish at a reasonable time, I don't spend too long away from home with my family. I make adjustments to my diary to go away on holidays and take annual leave. It was different in the first five or six years of my political career. I just burnt myself out completely and I suffered the consequences of that personally from failed relationships right the way through to my own personal physical and mental health. Maybe you have to learn that lesson the hard way, and I certainly have. But I have to say, I'm really pleased to be in a much better place now. You have to have that balance. If you don't, you will not just become all-consumed with your work, you will damage yourself and all those you love around you. It's really hard to describe the working environment of a minister unless you've been there, when, if you don't mind my French, the shit hits the fan. When it does, it is a very lonely place. Nobody else is invested in the issue you are dealing with as much as you. It's a really lonely environment. What drove me to overwork was a sense of having to prove myself doubly, because I was a minority and very young. I'm sure it's the same for women, I'm sure the same for people who have got a disability, maybe people who are gay feel it, maybe people with other protected characteristics. I felt I had to work twice as hard to prove myself after I was given a government job just one year into being elected. I thought I had to prove I was worthy of getting that job, and that it wasn't some kind of token gesture.

Losing a Seat

Elections inevitably result in some new members being elected and others losing their seats. These swings are usually viewed in an impersonal way, representing shifts in the popularity of different parties, changes in government or adjustments to the political balance in the chamber. Beneath these larger concerns, there are individuals whose lives are abruptly changed overnight, losing their prestigious jobs to become private citizens once more. Iain Gray, who was defeated in 2003 before returning to the Parliament in 2007, and Jamie Stone, who stood down ahead of the 2011 election in which his party was badly beaten, reflect on this experience of loss.

IAIN GRAY, Labour Party MSP and Former Scottish Labour Leader

I was devastated when I lost my seat in 2003, I didn't really see it coming. Some of those working on my campaign had been concerned, so I wasn't completely unprepared for it. But it is very abrupt. One minute you're a politician, the next minute you aren't. I found it really difficult to adjust to. My recollection is that I spent a lot of time looking for jobs. My wife's recollection is that I sat around in the house and did nothing. She's probably right and I'm probably wrong. It took me a few months to really pick myself up and start to seriously look for a job, and I did find one in the electronics industry. I was going to take it up, but just at that point Alistair Darling was made Secretary of State for Scotland and asked me if I would be his Special Advisor so I could inform him on the Scottish Parliament and devolution. So, I stayed in politics, just not as a politician. It wasn't the same. Especially given that I had been a government minister. I wasn't made to feel like a jumped-up bag carrier, I still felt at the centre of things, I was still in meetings where decisions were being taken and I felt treated as an equal. But it was a step down, even if it didn't feel like a massive one.

JAMIE STONE, Former Liberal Democrat MSP

Losing my seat wasn't as hard for me as it was for some others, because I stepped down on my own volition before the election. But it's pretty brutal what happens. All your privileges just go overnight, your ID card, the email account, everything goes. You are Mr Ordinary Bloke on the street. I remember John Farquhar Munro saying to me, 'Ah well, you'll find out what they really think of you now'. And that's dead right, you really do find out what they think of you. It was misery for some of my colleagues. I mean, some are almost basket cases because it is so utterly deflating. You are at the top of your game one moment and then your seat's gone and you're knackered. What do you do now? It is the ultimate flattening experience. I remember when I stood down from Holyrood, I was going into Lidl at home and I heard an old wifey saying to her husband, 'Oh look! That's Jimmie Stone, are you seeing him?' And he just said, 'Aye, it used to be'. That really struck me. I saw the funny side eventually, but for a moment I thought, 'You're nothing now, pal'. It was weird.

Generational Change and the Parliament Staff

A substantial part of the SPCB's staff body joined the Parliament in its first few years, a number of them in 1999 or even earlier, and have remained with it ever since. The generally pleasant working environment, especially once the worst of the troubles in the early days had passed, the good employment terms on offer and crucially the sense of mission many enjoy through their work as the heart of Scottish democracy, have meant that staff turnover has been very low throughout the Parliament's history. A comparatively small number of individuals have chosen to leave, with few new workers coming into the Parliament as a result. A large portion of these individuals were relatively young when the Parliament opened, contributing to the vibrant and chaotic atmosphere of the time, and have aged alongside the institution as a whole. While this has allowed the Parliament to build up a reservoir of highly experienced workers, it has left it cut off from the new blood that might have refreshed its energy, ideas and outlook.

David McGill admits that this situation developed almost absent-mindedly over the years, with the Parliament only moving to address it recently. The most visible step the Parliament has taken is its Modern Apprenticeship scheme, opening in 2014. This scheme provided an avenue for a small but ever growing contingent of young people to enter the Parliament's staff force. While this has created an unusual age dynamic in some instances, with a large generational divide separating the cohort of staff from the early days and the very young new recruits with few individuals in between, it has succeeded in shifting the wider profile of the Parliament. It has also had a visible benefit to the lives of those individuals who have been recruited through it, an experience that James Brown testifies to.

DAVID MCGILL, SPCB Assistant Chief Executive

A large portion of our staff have been here since the beginning. That has positive and negative impacts. The positives are obvious, we have got a staff group who are steeped in the knowledge of what they do, what the requirements of the law on them are, what services they need to provide, what the expectations of elected members are, and all that. And we have some real expertise in lots of fields. People come to us from around the world for information on strategic planning, and especially on scrutiny. That's because we have got 20 years of solid experience. The downsides are the risks of stagnation, the risks of becoming institutionalised, the risk of having a workforce that is not as diverse as we would like it to be. That is something that we have become aware of, and have sought to challenge. A few years ago, someone pointed out to us that we didn't have a single employee under the age of 24 on our books. That's not sustainable. Because we had so much focus, first on establishing the Parliament, then on the building project, then on settling into Holyrood and fine tuning ourselves, it took a long time for us to think more strategically about the organisation and make longer term plans. Now, we have begun a push to improve our demographics and to improve representation. So, although we get strong institutional benefits from having a stable workforce, we do recognise that we need to diversify and get the benefits of perspective from all walks of life.

JAMES BROWN, SPCB Administrator

Before I came here, I volunteered with a youth work charity, I had been doing that since I was 15. When the independence referendum came about, everybody in Scotland was speaking about it. It was on the telly, it was everywhere. That was when I started to pay attention and realised that I could understand all of the political language, the way the Parliament works, the way it works down south in Westminster, and it just clicked into gear as if it was second nature to me. I was doing health and social care at college, and one of the women that worked there emailed me saying, 'You should look at this thing that the Parliament is about to launch'. I had a look at it and thought there was absolutely no chance that a boy from Milton in Glasgow was going to get an apprenticeship with the Parliament. I just wrote an application thinking I would give it a bash. It came down to the last hour before the deadline, and I thought, 'Right, I'm doing this'. I sent my application in, got through to the next stage and went step by step through to working here. In the Modern Apprenticeship, you get thrown in at the deep end. I'd never experienced anything like this, and I had to engage with Assistant Chief Executives and people that are high up. I liked that. I think we've helped change the way the Parliament works. We're younger, we're more comfortable with technology, we've helped modernise everything.

I love working here, it's probably one of the best places in Scotland to work. Where else can you walk in to a building like this? I'm in the attic of Queensberry House and my desk looks across Arthur's Seat and Our Dynamic Earth. All my pals work in building sites as brickies or labourers, staying out in the pouring rain building scaffolding. I can't imagine a time where I don't want to work here, I love it. I would be lying if I never said that it changed my life. I always wanted to get away from staying in a scheme and working the same job, day in and day out, being in the pouring rain, being a labourer all day or whatever. Because that's where I would have been if I had not had this opportunity. So, the fact that I've actually managed to come from a scheme, and that comes with stuff all through your life, to get to a point where I can work in the Parliament, move to a different city, see a different part of the world and have a full-time job, it worked wonders for me and it has changed my life. I would say if you asked almost every apprentice that came through my batch, the apprentices would say the exact same thing. I think that's why the Modern Apprenticeship works wonders, because it does literally change lives.

Changes in the Media

The media are a core component of the Scottish Parliament's work. They provide scrutiny of the government and politicians in a way no other group can, and form the conduit through which the public is informed about the functioning of their democracy. Without them, this knowledge would be largely reserved for political insiders alone. The nation's political press has a very different appearance to that which welcomed into existence, and for a time terrified, the new Scottish Parliament two decades ago. Technological development has tremendously increased the importance of internet news sites, blogs and social media. This has been accompanied by a dramatic shift in consumer tastes away from the printed press, with newspaper sales having declined catastrophically since the 1990s and continuing to drop year-on-year across the industry. The past decade in particular has also witnessed a rise in public scepticism, and even outright distrust, of traditional news outlets. This landscape is far less established and secure than the situation that preceded it, offering a host of challenges to the press as it seeks to fulfil its important role into the future.

Journalists Brian Taylor and Katrine Bussey discuss these changes, their impact on different sections of the media and on the politics of the Parliament.

BRIAN TAYLOR, BBC Scottish Political Editor

The media has changed in the past 20 years. The power of the written press has declined somewhat, as a factor of falling circulation, social media has gained in importance, but without weakening the reach of broadcasting. We still have very large viewing and listening figures for BBC programmes, we still have a very large reach. There are still large numbers who tune in to the BBC radio and television programmes or check out the BBC website. Social media has to some extent changed the nature of journalism. It has become a key source for the written press, and occasionally broadcasters and radio as well. It has been used as a source to build stories around. But I don't think it is remotely an exclusive source, anyone can see it. It may have depressed newspaper circulations, but I think that was going to happen anyway as a result of broadcasting and the delay it takes in bringing papers to market.

Today, people are not really prepared to wait that long for news when they can look at the internet or social media and read it instantly.

KATRINE BUSSEY, Press Association Scotland Political Editor

There are a lot of people who don't trust the media nowadays. As a journalist, you can get a lot of flak from people who are very committed on one side of the debate or another. There are a lot of pro-independence supporters who don't trust the media because it hasn't supported them in the past, there's a lot of Jeremy Corbyn supporters who don't support the mainstream media because it hasn't always been favourable to him either, and so on. When you turn up at jobs, at a speech or a rally, you will often sit among the activists and punters and you can see people looking at you and muttering away about the mainstream media and lies. I just like to focus on the job of reporting what happens. I think this is something that has become more prominent in recent years. It was in the run-up to the 2014 independence referendum that we really saw this distrust of the media take hold. It's continued on since then.

This distrust has led some people towards other sources, like new media websites and bloggers for their information. I think there are questions over how reliable the writers on these websites are. I think there are questions over how reliable they are as journalists. I don't know if everybody who sets up or writes for a website has been trained in journalism, but everybody who works at the Press Association, and all the other journalists in the Parliament, have been. Sometimes these websites have become controversial, and become the story in themselves, most prominently Wings Over Scotland. Until very recently, most of these sort of websites in Scotland have been pro-SNP. The other parties have been slower to realise that they are missing out on a way of getting information to a large group of their supporters. Another change has been that the likes of Twitter and Facebook now allow politicians to talk directly to the public. They don't need to speak through people in the media anymore. This is all a part of a changing society, you can't expect everything to stay the same. But the media do still get access to politicians. The way it happens has changed and the level of access has changed, but we still get access that others don't. We've gone through a massive change in the news industry, which has seen the decline of print-based media and the growth of social media and online publishing.

PART 4

Gàidhlig anns a' Phàrlamaid
Gaelic in the Parliament

Translated by Alasdair MacCaluim

Gàidhlig anns a' Phàrlamaid

Tha suidheachadh air leth aig a' Ghàidhlig ann an coimhearsnachd na h-Alba. An-diugh, cha bhi ach beag-chuid de dh'Albannaich a' tuigsinn a' chànain ann an dòigh sam bith. Bidh mu 1 sa cheud den t-sluagh ga bruidhinn gu fileanta, agus bidh nas lugha na 2 sa cheud ag ràdh gu bheil comas sam bith aca sa chànan. Tha UNESCO ga rangachadh mar gu deimhinnte fo chunnart, aig riosga de dhol à bith gu tur. Ach tha an cànan cudromach mar shamhla airson Alba gu ìre tòrr nas motha na thuigeadh daoine bho na h-àireamhan sin a-mhàin. Gu h-eachdraidheil, bha i air a bruidhinn air feadh pàirt mhòr de dh'Alba, agus b' i cànan mòr-chuid na dùthcha aig aon àm. Gus an latha an-diugh, bidh i air a cleachdadh gu tric ann an grunn choimhearsnachdan air a' Ghàidhealtachd agus sna h-Eileanan, agus tha na mìltean dhiubhsan aig a bheil Gàidhlig bhon ghlùn agus a dh'ionnsaich i mar inbhich sgapte air feadh a' chòrr den dùthaich cuideachd. Tha mòran den bheachd gu bheil an cànan na phàirt bhunaiteach de dh'fhèin-aithne agus eachdraidh na h-Alba san fharsaingeachd agus airson na Gàidhealtachd gu h-àraid, agus gu bheil e mar dhleastnas air an dùthaich an cànan a ghleidheadh. Tha dealas mòr aig feadhainn eile airson taic a thoirt do choimhearsnachd Ghàidhlig a chaidh a dhearmad agus a dhroch-làimhseachadh leis na h-ùghdarrasan fad ghinealaichean, le bhith a' toirt dhaibh, airson a' chiad uair riamh, an aon chothrom air an stàit tron Ghàidhlig 's a tha aig luchd na Beurla a tha nam mòr-chuid.

'S e Alasdair MacCaluim fear den phrìomh luchd-obrach a bhios a' brosnachadh a' chànain sa Phàrlamaid. Tha esan a' mìneachadh an àite a tha aig a' chànan sa bhuidhinn, agus tha e a' beachdachadh air mar a tha beachdan mun Ghàidhlig air atharrachadh rè ùine agus mar a tha i a-nis nas fhollaisich tro cheumannan reachdail agus tro aithneachadh a tha nas neo-fhoirmeil.

ALASDAIR MACCALUIM, Oifigear Leasachaidh na Gàidhlig aig Buidheann Chorporra Pàrlamaid na h-Alba

Thug Pàrlamaid na h-Alba deagh chothrom dhuinn beachdachadh air a' Ghàidhlig. Mus do thòisich mi an seo, bha beagan shoidhnichean ann agus chaidh a' chiad deasbad a chumail mun Ghàidhlig ann an 2000. Tha mi a' smaoineachadh gur e rud fìor chudromach a bh' anns an deasbad sin, oir b' e sin a chiad turas a bhruidhinn a' Phàrlamaid mu inbhe na Gàidhlig agus mun Ghàidhlig san fharsaingeachd ann an doimhneachd. Bha tòrr deagh rùn ann agus bhruidhinn tòrr de na buill ann – cuid aig nach robh Gàidhlig ach a bha ag iarraidh beagan fheuchainn, agus bhruidhinn feadhainn a bha fileanta tòrr Gàidhlig. Tha mi a' smaoineachadh gur e àm ro-chudromach airson na Gàidhlig a bh' ann agus gun tug e ìre de dh'aithneachadh dhi. Ann an Westminster, tha an uiread aca ri dèiligeadh ris, agus cha robh ann an gnothaichean na h-Alba ach pàirt gu math beag de sin, agus fiù 's le deagh rùn, cha b' urrainn dhaibh mòran aire a thoirt dhan Ghàidhlig.

Nuair a thàinig mi an seo ann an 2002, bha beagan faicsinneachd aig a' Ghàidhlig, bha beagan ghoireasan air-loidhne ann agus bhiodh a' Phàrlamaid a' bruidhinn air cùisean na Gàidhlig. Ach aig an aon àm, cha robh poileasaidh Gàidhlig ann. Gach turas a bha thu ag iarraidh rudeigin a dhèanamh, bhiodh an aon argamaid ann: 'Carson a tha sinn a' dèanamh seo sa Ghàidhlig?'. Uaireannan, bha mì-rùn ann: 'Carson idir a dhèanamaid seo? Tha Beurla aig a h-uile duine co-dhiù.' Bhiodh an argamaid sin ann gu tric. Tha an nàimhdeas sin air crìonadh gu ìre mhòr gu cinnteach. Nuair a thàinig mi an seo an toiseach, chaidh innse dhomh turas no dhà nach robh mi an seo gus Gàidhlig a leasachadh, gum b' urrainn dhomh seirbheisean a thoirt seachad sa Ghàidhlig ach nach bu chòir dhomh rud sam bith a dhèanamh a bhiodh a' leasachadh a' chànain.

Thug Achd na Gàidhlig 2005 cruth-atharrachadh air cùisean. An àite a bhith a' faighneachd am bu chòir dhuinn a' Ghàidhlig a bhrosnachadh, bha sinn a-nis a' bruidhinn air ciamar a bu chòir dhuinn a dhèanamh. Thug e soilleireachadh dhuinn air na bha sinn a' feuchainn ri dhèanamh agus rinn sin eadar-dhealachadh mòr. Bha e cuideachd math a thaobh eachdraidh a' chànain, oir bha daoine air a bhith ag iomairt airson tomhas de dh'inbhe oifigeil fad 100 bliadhna no mar sin agus bha an iomairt air a bhith gu math gnìomhach bho dheireadh nan 90an. Bha buidhnean poblach eile a' sgrìobhadh phlanaichean cuideachd agus, mar sin, bha e a' fàs na b' fhasa rudan a dhèanamh a thaobh na Gàidhlig. Cha b' e dìreach sinne aig a' Phàrlamaid a bh' ann, ach Riaghaltas na h-Alba, ùghdarrasan ionadail, grunnan NDPBs agus mar sin air adhart. Bha e mar phàirt de ghluasad nas fharsainge. Uaireannan, nuair a tha thu air thoiseach air càch, tha dragh ort gum bi thu a' coimhead gòrach, gun tèid do chàineadh. Mar sin, bha e na b' fhasa gun robh daoine eile ga dhèanamh aig an aon àm, gun robh na bha sinn a' dèanamh a' fàs nas àbhaistiche agus gum b' urrainn dhuinn leantainn oirnn le bhith a' gluasad air adhart leis a' Ghàidhlig.

A-nis, tha sinn air cur ri faicsinneachd agus tha sinn comasach air tòrr diofar sheirbheisean a thoirt seachad sa Ghàidhlig agus tha sua-icheantas dà-chànanach Beurla is Gàidhlig againn. Roimhe sin, bha suaicheantasan Gàidhlig is Beurla fa leth ann agus is gann gum bi-odh duine sam bith a' faicinn an tionndaidh Ghàidhlig. Tha sinn a' cur cuideam air na meadhanan sòisealta agus a' feuchainn ri cur ri ìre cleachdaidh nan seirbheisean. Tha tòrr deagh rùn agus taic ann dhan Ghàidhlig ach gu tric, tha againn ri ràdh, 'O, an do smaoinich thu air seo a dhèanamh sa Ghàidhlig?'. Bidh daoine a' dìochuimhneachadh mu dei-dhinn. Tha sinn air a bhith feuchainn ri dhèanamh cinnteach gum bi sinn mar phàirt de na pròiseasan pàrlamaideach.

'S e a' chùis as motha dhuinn a bhith a' feuchainn ri toirt air daoine Gàidhlig a chleachdadh. Tha tòrr daoine aig a bheil Gàidhlig nach eil a' faireachdainn brosnachail mu bhith a' dèiligeadh ri buidhnean po-blach sa chànan. Tha tòrr dhaoine ann, mar as trice daoine nas sine, aig a bheil Gàidhlig fìor fhileanta bho thùs ach nach bi ga sgrìobhadh agus nach bi ga cleachdadh airson bruidhinn ri buidhnean poblach. Tha seo dìreach mar thoradh air mar a bha an comann sòisealta ag obair san àm a dh'fhalbh. Ann an coimhearsnachdan traidiseanta na Gàidhlig, chan eil an stàit riamh air cothrom a thoirt do dhaoine a bhith a' conaltradh rithe sa Ghàidhlig. Mar sin, chaidh a' Ghàidhlig a chleachdadh airson an teaghlaich, na dachaigh agus na coimhearsnachd, chan ann airson a bhith a' dèiligeadh ri buidhnean riaghaltais, agus tha e doirbh sin athar-rachadh. A bharrachd air seo, ged a tha an fheadhainn nas òige a chaidh tro fhoghlam tro mheadhan na Gàidhlig nas brosnachaile mun Ghàidh-lig, 's e a' Bheurla a th' aca bho thùs gu tric agus tha iad air Gàidhlig ionnsachadh san sgoil. Mar sin, tha e gu tric nas fhasa dhaibh Beurla a chleachdadh.

Bidh sinn a' coimhead air dùthchannan eile – a' Chuimrigh is Èirinn agus iomadh àite eile aig a bheil mion-chànan. 'S e an duilgheadas a th' againn gu bheil suidheachadh eadar-dhealaichte aig a' Ghàidhlig bhon mhòr-chuid aca. Anns a' Chuimrigh, tha barrachd luchd-labhairt ann agus cultar de dhà-chànanas. Ann an Èirinn, 's i a' Ghaeilge prìomh chànan oifigeil na stàite agus tha inbhe àrd aice. Tha iad a' cleachdadh a' chànain barrachd sna pàrlamaidean aca. Tha àiteachan eile ann mar Eilean Mhanainn, Deàrsaidh is Geàrnsaidh far am bi iad a' cleachdadh beagan den chànan air adhbharan samhlachail. Dh'fhaoidte gun cleachd buill an sin abairt an siud 's an seo ann an Gàidhlig Mhanainn fiù 's mur eil iad fileanta. Tha sinn a' feuchainn ri modail de dhà-chànanas a lorg a tha ag obair airson Pàrlamaid na h-Alba. Tha a' Ghàidhlig fìor chudromach airson Alba gu samhlachail, ach chan eil àireamh mhòr de luchd-labhairt aice no de bhuill phàrlamaid aig a bheil i. Mar sin, tha sinn air tòrr rudan a dhèanamh a tha samhlachail agus nì sinn ar dìcheall gum bi e cho furasta 's a ghabhas a' Ghàidhlig a chleachdadh còmhla ruinn. Aig an aon àm, chan eil sinne coltach ris a' Chuimrigh no Èirinn far am bi iad ag eadar-theangachadh an reachdais. Cha b' fhiach sin, oir chan eil daoine gu leòr ann a leughadh e. Tha sinn daonnan airson ionnsachadh bho dheagh chleachdadh aig taighean-reachdais is buidhnean poblach eile, ge b' e far a bheil iad – agus tha mi fhathast an dòchas gum faigh sinn cuireadh gu Reachdadaireachd Stàit Hawai'i latha de na làithean!

Mhothaich mi gu bheil an dòigh anns a bheilear a' coimhead air a' Ghàidhlig air atharrachadh san àm bhon reifreann air neo-eisimeileachd. Tha tòrr de na daoine a tha an aghaidh na Gàidhlig ga faicinn mar rudeigin a tha gu math poilitigeach agus dlùth-cheangailte ri nàiseantachd na h-Alba. Ach chan eil coimhearsnachd na Gàidhlig mar sin, chan eil iad ga faicinn mar sin agus chan eil na beachdan poilitigeach aca diofraichte ri beachdan muinntir na h-Alba gu ìre mhòr sam bith. Tha e a' cur orm gun can cuid gu bheil a' Ghàidhlig poilitigeach; tha mise a' smaoineachadh gu bheil a' Ghàidhlig airson a h-uile duine. Tha daoine mar mi fhìn a tha an sàs ann an leasachadh na Gàidhlig airson 's gun ionnsaich daoine Gàidhlig, ge b' e dè an cinneadh, poileataics, dath no creideamh a th' aca. Tha sinn a' smaoineachadh gur ann a h-uile duine a tha a' Ghàidhlig.

Gaelic in the Parliament

The place of the Gaelic language has a unique position within Scottish society. Today, only a small minority of Scots have any understanding of the language. Around one per cent of the population speak it fluently, with less than two per cent claiming to have any level of Gaelic-language ability. UNESCO categories it as 'definitively endangered', at risk of disappearing entirely. However, its symbolic importance to Scotland far outweighs what these numbers might infer. Historically, it was spoken over a large part of Scotland, at one point being the nation's majority language. To this day, it is used widely in a small number of communities in the Highlands and Islands, with thousands of native-speakers and adult learners spread through the rest of the country. For many, the language is seen as an integral part of the identity and history of Scotland in general and the Highlands in particular, whose preservation is a national duty. Others have a passionate desire to provide support to a Gaelic-speaking community that has been neglected and ill-treated by authorities for generations, giving them the same access to the state as the English-speaking majority for the first time.

One of the key figures in promoting the language in the Parliament, Alasdair MacCaluim, describes its role within the institution, observing the way in which attitudes towards it have developed over time and its presence has increased through legislative measures and less formal recognition.

ALASDAIR MACCALUIM, SPCB Gaelic Development Officer

The Scottish Parliament provided a good opportunity to discuss Gaelic. Before I started, we had some signage and there was the first debate about Gaelic in 2000. I think that debate was a key moment, because it was the first time that people were talking about the status of Gaelic and about Gaelic in general in the Parliament. There was a huge amount of goodwill and a lot of members spoke, a lot of members who weren't Gaelic speakers had a go and the ones that were fluent spoke a lot of Gaelic. I think that was a great turning point for the Gaelic community, it gave it a certain degree of acceptance. In Westminster, they had so much to deal with, and Scottish affairs were only a small part of that. With all the goodwill in the world, they weren't going to give it much attention. So, when I arrived here in 2002, the Parliament had some visibility of

Gaelic, some web resources and it was already discussing Gaelic issues. But at the time there wasn't a Gaelic policy. Every time you wanted to do something in Gaelic you would have to go through the same argument, 'Why are we doing this in Gaelic?' Occasionally, you'd get some hostility, 'What's the point? Everybody speaks English anyway'. You had that argument a lot. That hostility has definitely faded. When I first came here, I was told a couple of times that I wasn't here to develop Gaelic, I could provide services but I wasn't to do anything promoting the language.

The Gaelic Language Act in 2005 was a game changer. Instead of asking if we should promote Gaelic, it shifted the conversation to how we should do it. It clarified what we were trying to achieve, that made a huge difference. It was also great for the history of the language, because people had been campaigning for some type of official status for about 100 years, and very actively from the late 1990s. Other public bodies were drawing up plans too, so it was becoming easier to get Gaelic things done. It wasn't just us at the Parliament, it was the Scottish Government, it was local authorities, it was various NDPBs and so on. It was part of an overarching expansion. Sometimes when you are ahead of the curve you can feel lonely, you're worried that you might look daft, you might be criticised. So, the fact that other people were doing it at the same time meant we were getting more mainstream and could keep moving forward.

Now we've managed to increase visibility, we've managed to provide a lot of services, we have a bilingual logo for the Parliament that is in both English and Gaelic. Previously, there were separate English and Gaelic logos, but the Gaelic one was almost never seen. We are now putting a lot of emphasis on social media and trying to encourage uptake. There's a lot of goodwill for Gaelic, lots of support, but quite often we'd find ourselves saying, 'Oh, did you think about doing this in Gaelic?' People forget about it. We've been trying to make sure that we are included in processes within the Parliament.

The bigger issue for us is trying to get people to use Gaelic. A lot of Gaelic speakers don't feel confident in dealing with the public bodies in the language. Quite a lot of the older people speak Gaelic very fluently, it's their first language, but they never used it in writing, and won't speak to public bodies in it. That is just because of the way society worked in the past. In the traditional Gaelic speaking areas, the state has never really let people interact with it in Gaelic. So, Gaelic has always been used for family, home and community interactions, not for dealing with government bodies and it's hard to change that. On top of that, all the younger Gaelic speakers that have been through Gaelic-medium education, they are more confident about Gaelic, but English is their first language and they've learnt Gaelic at school. So, it's easier for them to use English.

We often look at other countries like Wales, Ireland and various other places that use minority languages. But the problem is that Gaelic has a different position from most of them. In Wales there are a lot more speakers and a bigger culture of bilingualism. In Ireland it is the first official language of the state, it has a high status. They use the language much more in their parliaments. Then there are a lot of other places like the Isle of Man, Jersey and Guernsey where they use a little of the language for ceremonial purposes. Members might use an expression here and there in Manx, even if they are not fluent in it. We are trying to find a model of bilingualism that works for the Scottish Parliament. Gaelic is very important symbolically for Scotland, but there are not a large number of speakers, or a large number of members who speak it. So, we've done a lot of things that are symbolic, and we try to make it as easy as possible for people to use Gaelic with us. But at the same time, we are not like Wales or Ireland where they translate the legislation. There just aren't enough people who would read it to make it worthwhile. We always want to see good practices from other legislatures and public bodies wherever they are. I am still hoping that we get invited to the Hawaiian State Legislature!

I have noticed that the way Gaelic is looked at has changed since the independence referendum. A lot of people who are against Gaelic see it as being very strongly political and very strongly associated with Scottish Nationalism. Whereas, the Gaelic community isn't like that, they don't see it as political and their political allegiances aren't significantly different to the people of Scotland in general. It is frustrating that you get people saying Gaelic is political, I think that Gaelic belongs to everybody. People like me that are involved in Gaelic development, want everybody to learn Gaelic regardless of their politics or race, colour or creed. We think of Gaelic as being something for everybody.

PART 5
The Scottish Parliament at 20

The Parliament's Report Card

Assessing the Scottish Parliament as it turns 20 is an exceptionally difficult task. It has been through a difficult journey to reach this point, establishing itself from scratch, suffering through deaths, resignations, scandals, and controversies of all kinds, not least over the Holyrood building, shifts in its constitutional foundations and the tumultuous churn of politics in an era of instability and change. It has met some of the ambitions of those who voted it into existence in 1997, and fallen short of others. It has made tangible contributions to Scottish life, without utterly transforming it. In some respects, it has become the focal point of the nation's politics, yet it is still often overshadowed by the larger United Kingdom Parliament at Westminster. The verdict each person will come to is entirely subjective. To conclude this volume, five individuals from an array of competing viewpoints – Jackson Carlaw, Jack McConnell, Mike Rumbles, Humza Yousaf and Brian Taylor – provide their own verdicts on the Parliament as it reaches towards its 20th anniversary.

JACKSON CARLAW, Conservative & Unionist Party MSP

I think the early ambitions for the Parliament were unrealistic. There was an idea that it would be a melting pot for the greatest and the best of Scotland. Well, no. You have to join a political party to get in here. The only Independent members were generally people who resigned from a party for whatever reason. That was one of the lofty ideals. They also thought that just by virtue of the fact we were taking the decisions in Scotland that we would be making better decisions. If they are better decisions, then they haven't had better outcomes in a lot of instances. So, I think some of the lofty ideals were ludicrous. On the other hand, it is a somewhat accessible Parliament, certainly more so than Westminster. It has become one of Scotland's biggest tourist attractions. If it's not full of schoolchildren, it's full of tourists or it's full of members of the public. I think that it has become an established part of Scotland's political life,

without necessarily resolving the tensions and problems that led to it being established in the first place.

JACK MCCONNELL, Former Labour Party MSP, Scottish La-
bour Leader and First Minister

Few outside of the Parliament think that the current Scottish Parliament
is anything like as challenging, exciting and visionary as it should be.
That isn't a comment on any one political party. It isn't the crisis of confidence in the Parliament as an institution like we had in the first couple
of years of the Parliament. But I think we now have a sense of resignation
about the quality of debate, and the level of substance, in the Parliament
amongst the general public. People absolutely accept the institution, they
look to it to lead Scotland. They look to it to reflect and represent Scotland and take us into the future. But I think there is a deep-seated sense
that it has not lived up to what it could be. It will be up to the current
generation of MSPs to address that.

MIKE RUMBLES, Liberal Democrat MSP

The Parliament has had a huge impact. I think the key issue has been
remoteness, the Parliament in London was seen as very distant from
Scotland. But people can come to visit the Scottish Parliament, see us
dealing with everyday issues that they can influence. Of course, some
parts of Scotland are far from Edinburgh, but it is not nearly as distant
as London. People from the North-East can go through to the Scottish
Parliament, carry out their business and go home, in a day. That wasn't
possible with Westminster. However, as a caveat, I noticed after I lost my
seat in 2011 that the Scottish Parliament doesn't resonate with the media
and public as much as we think in here. The political news you get is
mostly concerned with what is going on down in London. What we do
passes most people by. You'll find only a tiny amount of people are interested in First Minister's Questions. People often talk about a Westminster
bubble, but there is a Scottish Parliament bubble too.

HUMZA YOUSAF, Scottish National Party MSP

The Scottish Parliament has been utterly transformative. I don't think
our predecessors that voted for this Parliament in 1997 could have envisioned the difference it would make to Scottish public life. I have talked to
many individuals and organisations representing vulnerable groups over

the years, and their access to the political process now is incomparable to what they had before the creation of this Parliament. You can get a meeting with a minister within a matter of weeks. That access to government and parliamentarians wasn't possible before this Parliament. It has brought politics much closer to the Scottish people, right to their doorsteps. Regardless of who is in charge, we are much better off now that we have this place.

BRIAN TAYLOR, BBC Scottish Political Editor

Parliaments of all types broadly do three things if they are proper parliaments. They are lawmakers, they ventilate issues of concern to the people they are representing, and they hold the governing executive to account. I think that from the earliest days, the Scottish Executive, now the Scottish Government, were definitely held to account by Parliament in a way that the previous Scottish Office had been only sporadically by the likes of the Scottish select committee. They were suddenly held to account in a much more precise way. If a minister goes in and gets a bit of a kicking from a committee, then that you can be sure that minister is going to go back to the department and give a bit of a kicking to the civil service. The civil service will then respond to that by improving their game. So, I think that the scrutiny was excellent from the outset. The one thing that struck me the most was that the Parliament became a forum for pretty well every issue in Scottish domestic life, from the state of our health service to the state of our football team. Every issue eventually, and generally fairly quickly, found its way into the Parliament. It has also been accepted by the public that this is the forum in which the issues they are concerned with will be discussed. On law making, I think they've got the balance right now. In the early days they were a bit too eager to make laws for the sake of gesture. They have improved in that respect over time. The scrutiny of legislation has got better as well, although it can always be improved. I think that the Parliament has delivered what was expected of it, and what is expected of parliaments more generally.

Glossary of Terms

ABSOLUTE MAJORITY
When the number of members voting for a proposition is more than half of the total number of seats. In a Parliament with 129 seats, 65 votes would be required to obtain an absolute majority.

ACT
An Act creates a new law or changes an existing law.

ADDITIONAL MEMBER SYSTEM
The form of voting system used to elect the Scottish Parliament.

ALLOWANCES
Members expenses that can be claimed back from the Parliament.

AMENDMENTS
Proposed textual changes to motions or bills.

BACKBENCHER
Colloquial term, derived from Westminster, that is used to denote those MSPs who are not ministers, party leaders or party spokespersons. Sometimes also used of all MSPs other than ministers and Presiding Officers.

BILL
A draft Act introduced into Parliament.

BUDGET
The three-stage annual process for the parliamentary consideration of the Scottish Government's expenditure plans.

BUSINESS MANAGER
Colloquial term for the MSP appointed by his or her party leader to be that party's representative on the Parliamentary Bureau and to organise that party's contributions to debates and other parliamentary business. Equivalent to a 'chief whip' in Westminster.

BY-ELECTION
The method of filling a constituency vacancy arising during a parliamentary session through an election conducted only in that seat.

CABINET
The group of senior ministers of the Scottish Government appointed by the First Minister.

CHAMBER DESK
The section of the Chamber Office that processes, and advises on the processing of, parliamentary questions, motions and amendments to motions, and produces the Written Answers Report. In the House of Commons, parliamentary questions and motions are dealt with by the Table Office.

CIVIL SERVANTS
Officials of the executive arm of government.

CLERK
A Parliament official who provides procedural and administrative support to the Parliament or to a committee.

CLERK OF THE PARLIAMENT / CHIEF EXECUTIVE
The senior official of the Parliament's administration.

COALITION
A formal arrangement between two or more parties or groupings to combine to form a government.

CODE OF CONDUCT
A code of rules and guidance on standards of conduct by MSPs in carrying out their parliamentary duties.

COMMITTEE
A small group of MSPs formed to deal with particular parliamentary business.

COMMITTEE BILL
A public bill introduced by the convener of a committee.

COMMITTEE ROOMS
Rooms in the Parliament building used for committee meetings and other events.

CONFIDENCE OF THE PARLIAMENT
When a motion of no confidence is passed, stating that the Scottish Government no longer enjoys the confidence of the Parliament. All ministers are required to resign and the government is expected to dissolve.

CONSTITUENCY
An electoral area which elects a single MSP using the first-past-the-post system.

CONSTITUENCY MEMBER
An MSP elected using the first-past-the-post voting system for a constituency.

CONSTITUTIONAL CONVENTION
The body composed of a number of Scottish political parties and other public groups and organisations which, from 1989 until 1995, produced the detailed proposals for a devolution scheme which informed UK government policy from 1997.

CONSULTATIVE STEERING GROUP (CSG)
The group set up by the Secretary of State for Scotland in 1998 to bring together views on the Scottish Parliament and to consider the Parliament's operational needs and working methods. Its membership included representatives of the main Scottish political parties as well as a wide range of civic groups and interests. Its main report was published in January 1999.

CONVENER
The MSP who convenes and chairs a committee.

CORPORATE BODY
See *Scottish Parliamentary Corporate Body*

CROSS-PARTY GROUP (CPG)
A group made up of MSPs from across the parties and people from outside the Parliament who share an interest in a particular subject or issue.

DEBATES
Discussions by MSPs, usually based on a motion.

DEBATING CHAMBER
The place for meetings of the Parliament.

DECISION TIME
The period at the end of a day's business in the Parliament when decisions are taken by MSPs in the chamber on most of the questions before it.

DEPUTY FIRST MINISTER
A non-statutory term for the Cabinet Minister who is deputy to the
First Minister.

DEPUTY PRESIDING OFFICERS
The Presiding Officer's two deputies, who can also preside at the Parliament's meetings and undertake other functions of the Presiding Officer. They can participate in proceedings and can vote on the same basis as other MSPs when not chairing a meeting.

DEVOLUTION
The process of decentralising the governance of Scotland, within the UK, from the central authorities in Westminster and Whitehall to a Scottish Parliament and Government. Similar schemes have been implemented for Northern Ireland and Wales.

DEVOLVED MATTERS
Matters for which the Scottish Parliament and/or the Scottish Government have responsibility.

DIVISION
The means for deciding a question, other than by consensus, by MSPs voting in the chamber.

DUAL MANDATE
The term used to describe those MSPs who, in addition to their seat in the Scottish Parliament, also hold a seat in either the House of Commons, House of Lords or represent a ward in their local council.

EMERGENCY BILL
An Executive bill which, with the Parliament's agreement, undergoes a faster legislative process.

FINAL STAGE
The stage for final consideration of a private bill and a decision on whether it should be passed.

FIRST MINISTER
The head of the Scottish Executive or Scottish Government.

FIRST MINISTER'S QUESTIONS
A period when MSPs ask questions of the First Minister at a meeting of the Parliament, similar to Prime Minister's Questions in the House of Commons.

FIRST-PAST-THE-POST
Voting system where the candidate who obtains the largest number of votes in a given constituency is elected.

FRONTBENCHER
A colloquial term to denote those MSPs who are ministers or the spokespersons of opposition parties.

GARDEN LOBBY
The main thoroughfare which joins all the buildings in the Holyrood Parliament complex together.

GENERAL ELECTION
An election in which a poll is held for all 129 seats in the Parliament.

GOVERNMENT
The executive body that administers the running of the country.

GROUP
A group can be formed of members who represent parties with fewer than five seats in the Parliament, or of Independent members. The group must have at least five members, and is entitled to nominate a representative as a member of the Parliamentary Bureau.

HOLYROOD
The area of Edinburgh where the Scottish Parliament is located. Colloquially used when referring to the post-2004 Parliament itself.

HOLYROOD PROGRESS GROUP
A group that was set up following a resolution of the Parliament on 5 April 2000. It met for the first time in July 2000 and the last meeting was on 6 October 2004. Made

up of representatives of the Parliament and relevant professionals, it was directed to work with the SPCB to finalise the design of the new Parliament building, complete the project and report regularly to the SPCB and members on the progress and costs of construction.

HOLYROOD PROJECT TEAM
The group that acted as the SPCB's representative in securing delivery of the Scottish Parliament's new building at Holyrood.

HOME RULE
Another description for forms of democratically elected Scottish self-government, such as devolution.

HOUSE OF COMMONS
The lower house of the United Kingdom Parliament, composed of members of Parliament or MPs.

HOUSE OF LORDS
The upper house of the United Kingdom Parliament, composed of peers.

LAW OFFICERS
The senior legal advisers to the government.

LEADER OF THE OPPOSITION
An informal term sometimes applied to the leader of the largest non-government party in the Scottish Parliament.

LEGISLATION
Any written law agreed to and given authority by a law-making body.

LEGISLATIVE PROCESS
The stages of parliamentary consideration that a bill must go through to become an Act.

LIST MEMBER
An informal term for a regional MSP, derived from the party lists used for their election.

LOBBYING
Lobbying is when an individual or a group tries to persuade someone in Parliament to support a particular policy or campaign. Lobbying can be done in person, by sending letters and emails or via social media.

MEDIA RELATIONS OFFICE
The Media Relations Office is the office responsible for promoting the wide-ranging work of the Scottish Parliament, providing journalists with up-to-date information on the Committees, Chamber business, the work of the SPCB and the public engagement activities undertaken by the Parliament. The team also supports the accreditation system for journalists and other media personnel whose work requires access to the Scottish Parliament.

MEDIA TOWER
The building providing office accommodation to journalists at the Parliament.

MEETING OF THE PARLIAMENT
A gathering of the whole Parliament in the Debating Chamber.

MEMBER OF THE SCOTTISH EXECUTIVE OR SCOTTISH GOVERNMENT
The First Minister, ministers and the two Scottish Law Officers.

MEMBER OF THE SCOTTISH PARLIAMENT (MSP)
Person elected to the Scottish Parliament to represent a constituency or region.

MEMBER'S BILL
A public bill, other than a committee bill, introduced by an MSP who is not a member of the Scottish Executive.

MINISTER
A member of the government.

MOTION
A proposition considered and often decided upon by the Parliament or a committee.

MP
Member of the House of Commons.

OATH OF ALLEGIANCE

On being returned as members, all MSPs are required either to take the oath of allegiance or make the solemn affirmation before the Clerk at a meeting of the Parliament. An MSP may not participate in any other proceedings of the Parliament until he or she has taken the oath or made the solemn affirmation. An MSP that does not do this, normally within a two month period of being returned as an MSP, will cease to be an MSP.

OFFICIAL REPORT

The Official Report is the written record of what is said in public meetings of the Scottish Parliament and its committees.

OPPOSITION

A term commonly applied to those parties and groups in the Parliament that are not in the government.

ORAL QUESTION

A parliamentary question lodged for oral answer either at Question Time, First Minister's Question Time or SPCB Question Time.

PARLIAMENTARY BUREAU

The body consisting of the Presiding Officer and a representative of each party or grouping that has at least five members.

PARLIAMENTARY SERVICE

See *Scottish Parliamentary Service*

PARLIAMENTARY QUESTION

One means by which MSPs can seek information or explanation from ministers or the Scottish Parliamentary Corporate Body. Questions can be for oral or written answer.

PASSAGE OF A BILL

The process through which a bill passes from introduction into law.

POINT OF ORDER

An intervention by an MSP during parliamentary proceedings, questioning whether proper procedures have been followed or are being followed.

PRESIDING OFFICER
The MSP elected to chair meetings of the Parliament, the Parliamentary Bureau and the SPCB and to represent the Parliament externally.

RECESS
A period when the Parliament is not dissolved, but is not meeting for a particular length of time.

REGION
An electoral area which contains a number of Scottish parliamentary constituencies.

REGIONAL MEMBER
An MSP returned for one of the eight electoral regions in Scotland.

RESERVED MATTERS
Matters on which the UK Parliament at Westminster alone can pass valid legislation.

SCOTLAND ACT 1998
The main legislation of the UK Parliament, devolving powers to Scotland.

SCOTLAND ACT 2012
Amended the Scotland Act 1998, devolving further powers to Scotland influenced by the recommendations of the Calman Commission.

SCOTLAND ACT 2016
Amended the Scotland Act 1998, devolving further powers to Scotland through delivery of the recommendations of the Smith Commission.

SCOTTISH AFFAIRS COMMITTEE
A committee of the House of Commons appointed to examine the expenditure, administration and policy of the Scotland Office.

SCOTTISH EXECUTIVE
The Scottish Executive was the name for the Scottish Government between 1999 and 2007.

SCOTTISH GOVERNMENT
The Scottish Government is the group of ministers in the Scottish Government. It

comprises the First Minister, other senior ministers appointed by the First Minister and the two Scottish Law Officers. Informally, the term is frequently used to mean the senior ministers, the Scottish Law Officers, the junior ministers, and their staff. The Scottish Government is responsible for most of the issues of day-to-day concern to the people of Scotland, including health, education, justice, rural affairs, and transport.

SCOTTISH GRAND COMMITTEE
A standing committee of the House of Commons, consisting of all MPs for Scottish seats, together with some additional members. It has a range of functions under standing orders, from holding Ministers to account through questions and debates to scrutiny of certain types of Scottish legislation.

SCOTTISH OFFICE
The name of the former department of the UK government which dealt with many areas of Scottish government before devolution. Since the opening of the Scottish Parliament, it has been renamed the Scotland Office and possesses reduced powers.

SCOTTISH PARLIAMENTARY CORPORATE BODY (SPCB)
The body that arranges for the Parliament to be provided with staff, property and services.

SCOTTISH PARLIAMENTARY SERVICE
The Scottish Parliamentary Service is the collective term for the group of profession-al staff employed by the SPCB to support the business and operations of the Scottish Parliament.

SCOTTISH PARLIAMENTARY STANDARDS COMMISSIONER
The independent commissioner who investigates complaints that MSPs have breached the Code of Conduct.

SECRETARY OF STATE FOR SCOTLAND
The head of the Scotland Office, previously the Scottish Office, and the senior Min-ister of the UK Government dealing with Scottish matters.

SESSION
The period from the date of first meeting of the Parliament following a general election until it is dissolved prior to the next election. The parliament is currently in its fifth session.

SHADOW
An informal term for opposition frontbench posts or structures mirroring those in the government.

SHORT MONEY
An informal term for the scheme of assistance for registered non-government political parties in the Scottish Parliament.

SITTING DAY
A day when the Office of the Clerk is open and the Parliament is not in recess or dissolved.

SPECIAL ADVISER
A temporary civil servant appointed by the First Minister or the Deputy First Minister to advise ministers. Unlike permanent civil servants, special advisers do not have to behave with political impartiality, and must leave their posts if the First Minister or Deputy First Minister who appointed them leaves office. Equivalent posts exist in Westminster.

STAFF OF THE PARLIAMENT
The public servants provided by the SPCB for the Parliament's purposes.

STANDING ORDERS
The rules governing how the Parliament conducts its business.

STATUTORY INSTRUMENT
The main form for legislation made by ministers and others under powers delegated by an Act.

WESTMINSTER
The colloquial name for the UK Parliament, comprising the House of Commons and the House of Lords.

WHIP
A colloquial term, derived from Westminster parliamentary practice, for party business managers and others who fulfil the task of enforcing parliamentary party discipline in the Parliament.

WHITEHALL

The colloquial name for the UK government generally, and the civil service bureaucracy in particular.

WITNESS

A person invited or required to attend a meeting of a committee for the purpose of giving evidence.

Contributor Biographies

MSPS

WENDY ALEXANDER, SCOTTISH LABOUR PARTY

Wendy Alexander was a Special Advisor for Donald Dewar during his time as Secretary of State for Scotland between 1997 and 1999, before being elected as the Labour MSP for Paisley North from 1999 until 2011. She served as a member of the Scottish Executive between 1999 and 2002. After her party's defeat in the 2007 election, she became leader of the Scottish Labour Party in 2007, resigning the following year.

JACKIE BAILLIE, SCOTTISH LABOUR PARTY

Elected as the Labour MSP for Dumbarton in 1999, Jackie Baillie was briefly a minister in the Scottish Executive between 2000 and 2001. She has retained her Dumbarton constituency in every election since the advent of devolution.

DENNIS CANAVAN, INDEPENDENT

Dennis Canavan had a long career in the House of Commons, serving as the Labour MP for West Stirlingshire between 1974 and 1983 and Falkirk West between 1983 and 1999, continuing as the Independent MP for Falkirk West until 2000. After being denied the chance to stand for Falkirk West as a Labour candidate in the 1999 Scottish Parliamentary election, he won the seat as an Independent and represented the constituency until his retirement in 2007. He was subsequently the chair of the advisory board of Yes Scotland during the 2014 independence referendum.

JACKSON CARLAW, SCOTTISH CONSERVATIVE AND UNIONIST PARTY

After a long career as a senior party activist, Jackson Carlaw was elected to the Scottish Parliament as a Conservative MSP for the West of Scotland Region in 2007. In 2011, he became the Deputy Leader of the Scottish Conservative & Unionist Party, a position he retains to the present day. After several failed attempts, he became a constituency MSP after winning the Eastwood seat in the 2016 election.

LINDA FABIANI, SCOTTISH NATIONAL PARTY

Linda Fabiani entered the Scottish Parliament as an SNP MSP for the Central Scotland Region in 1999. She served in the Scottish Government for two years between 2007 and 2009 after her party won power. In 2011, she became the constituency MSP for East Kilbride. Since 2016, she has held the position of Deputy Presiding Officer.

RT HON SIR ALEX FERGUSSON, SCOTTISH CONSERVATIVE AND UNIONIST PARTY AND FORMER PRESIDING OFFICER
Alex Fergusson was elected as a Conservative MSP for the South Scotland Region in 1999, before becoming the member for Galloway and Upper Nithsdale in 2003. Between 2007 and 2011, he left the Conservative Party to take on the role of Presiding Officer. He re-joined the party for one final term in 2011, as the MSP for Galloway and West Dumfries. He retired from the Parliament in 2016, and passed away two years later in 2018.

MURDO FRASER, SCOTTISH CONSERVATIVE AND UNIONIST PARTY
Murdo Fraser has been a Conservative member for the Mid Scotland and Fife Region since 2001, after replacing the resigning Nick Johnston as an MSP. Between 2005 and 2011, he was the Deputy Leader of the Scottish Conservative & Unionist Party.

IAIN GRAY, SCOTTISH LABOUR PARTY
Iain Gray was the Labour MSP for Edinburgh Pentland from 1999 until his defeat in 2003. He then took on a role as an advisor to the Scottish Secretary Alistair Darling, before returning to the Parliament as the member for East Lothian in 2007. In 2008, he became the Leader of the Scottish Labour Party, resigning after his party's defeat in the 2011 election. He has subsequently remained a key figure within the Parliament's Labour group.

ROSS GREER, SCOTTISH GREEN PARTY
Ross Greer became the youngest member in the history of the Parliament after being elected as the Green MSP for West of Scotland Region in 2016.

ROBIN HARPER, SCOTTISH GREEN PARTY
Robin Harper was the first Green parliamentarian elected anywhere in the United Kingdom as the Green MSP for the Lothian Region in 1999. He was the Leader of the Scottish Green Party between 1999 and 2002, and its Co-Leader between 2004 and 2008. He retired from the Parliament in 2011.

FIONA HYSLOP, SCOTTISH NATIONAL PARTY
Fiona Hyslop entered the Parliament as an SNP MSP for the Lothian Region in 1999, and remained a list member until winning the Linlithgow constituency in 2011. Since 2007, she has served as a minister in the Scottish Government.

JOHANN LAMONT, SCOTTISH LABOUR PARTY
Johann Lamont was the Labour MSP for Glasgow Pollok between 1999 and 2016,

and has served as a member for the Glasgow Region since 2016. She led the Scottish Labour Party between 2011 and 2014, resigning shortly after the independence referendum.

RT HON KEN MACINTOSH, SCOTTISH LABOUR PARTY AND PRESIDING OFFICER

Ken Macintosh served as the Labour MSP for Eastwood from 1999 until 2016. He then became an MSP for the West of Scotland Region and Presiding Officer of the Scottish Parliament.

RT HON TRICIA MARWICK, SCOTTISH NATIONAL PARTY AND FORMER PRESIDING OFFICER

After serving as an SNP MSP for the Mid Scotland and Fife Region between 1999 and 2007, Tricia Marwick won the Central Fife constituency in 2007. In 2011, her constituency was redrawn as Mid Fife and Glenrothes, and she took on the role of Presiding Officer. She retired from politics in 2016.

JOHN MASON, SCOTTISH NATIONAL PARTY

John Mason was elected to the House of Commons in the 2008 Glasgow East by-election as an SNP MP, but lost his seat at the 2010 general election two years later. He has been an MSP in the Scottish Parliament since winning Glasgow Shettleston in 2011.

RT HON LORD JACK McCONNELL, SCOTTISH LABOUR PARTY

Having been a prominent figure in the party for years, Jack McConnell was elected as the Labour MSP for Motherwell and Wishaw in 1999, retaining his seat until standing down in 2011. He was a member of the Scottish Executive from 1999 until 2001, when he was elevated to the position of First Minister and Leader of the Scottish Labour Party. After his government secured re-election in 2003, he lost this position in 2007 as the Labour Party fell from power. His political career has continued in Westminster, where he has been a Peer in the House of Lords since 2010.

RT HON HENRY McLEISH, SCOTTISH LABOUR PARTY

Prior to his career in the Scottish Parliament, Henry McLeish was the Labour MP for Central Fife between 1987 and 2001. During that time, he played an important role in founding the Scottish Parliament as Minister of State for Scotland, a senior role in the Scottish Office between 1997 and 1999. In 1999, he became the MSP for Central Fife and a minister in the Scottish Executive. In 2000, he became First Minister and Leader of the Scottish Labour Party, following the death of Donald Dewar. He resigned one year later in 2001, and then left both the Parliament, and politics, behind in 2003 when he stood down from his seat.

ALEX NEIL, SCOTTISH NATIONAL PARTY

Alex Neil had been a key activist in a number of different political parties before his parliamentary career began when he was elected to represent the Central Scotland Region in 1999 for the SNP. In 2009, he became a member of the Scottish Government, and in 2011 won the Airdrie and Shotts constituency seat. He left the Scottish Government in 2016, but remains active in the Parliament as an MSP.

MIKE RUMBLES, SCOTTISH LIBERAL DEMOCRATS

Mike Rumbles was the Liberal Democrat MSP for West Aberdeenshire and Kincardine between 1999 and his electoral defeat in 2011. He returned to the Parliament as a member for the North East Scotland Region in 2016.

TAVISH SCOTT, SCOTTISH LIBERAL DEMOCRATS

Tavish Scott has been the Liberal Democrat MSP for Shetland since 1999. He served as a member of the Scottish Executive between 2000 and 2001, and again from 2003 until 2007. He became the Leader of the Scottish Liberal Democrats in 2008, and resigned in 2011 following the party's poor performance in that year's election, but remains active in the Parliament as an MSP.

TOMMY SHERIDAN, SCOTTISH SOCIALIST PARTY AND SOLIDARITY GROUP

Tommy Sheridan had been a major force in Scottish far-left politics for a decade before he became the Convener of the Scottish Socialist Party in 1998 and was elected as its first MSP in 1999, representing the Glasgow Region. He stood down as Convener of the SSP in 2004, and then left the party entirely in 2006. He then became the Co-convener of Solidarity, losing his seat in the Scottish Parliament in 2007. Nonetheless, he subsequently remained politically active outside of elected politics, remaining Solidarity's Co-convener until 2016.

RT HON LORD DAVID STEEL KT KBE PC, SCOTTISH LIBERAL DEMOCRATS AND
FORMER PRESIDING OFFICER

David Steel was the most politically experienced individual to make the move to the Scottish Parliament in 1999. He had first been elected to the House of Commons in 1965, at the time youngest sitting MP or Baby of the House, as the Liberal MP for Roxburgh, Selkirk & Peebles. Although boundary changes shifted his seat to Tweeddale, Ettrick & Lauderdale, he represented largely the same area in the Scottish Borders from 1965 through to his retirement from the Commons in 1997. During that time, he was the last Leader of the Liberal Party, guiding them through their Alliance with the Social Democratic Party between 1981 and 1988, and the eventual merger of the two parties into the Liberal Democrats in 1988. In 1999, he was elected to the Scottish Parliament as a member for the Lothians Region, and became its first Presiding Officer. After stepping down from the Parliament in 2003, he has remained involved in politics as a Peer in the House of Lords since 1997.

JAMIE STONE, SCOTTISH LIBERAL DEMOCRATS

Jamie Stone was the Liberal Democrat MSP for Caithness, Sutherland and Easter Ross between 1999 and 2011, standing down prior to that election. He returned to parliamentary politics in 2017 as the MP for Caithness, Sutherland and Easter Ross in the House of Commons.

JOHN SWINNEY, SCOTTISH NATIONAL PARTY

John Swinney served as the SNP MP for Tayside North from 1997 until 2001. He arrived in the Scottish Parliament in 1999 as the MSP of North Tayside, representing largely the same area under changed boundaries as Perthshire North since 2011. Between 2000 and 2004, he was the Leader of the Scottish National Party. He has been a senior figure in the Scottish Government since 2007, and the Deputy First Minister since 2014.

RT HON LORD JIM WALLACE QC, SCOTTISH LIBERAL DEMOCRATS AND FORMER DEPUTY FIRST MINISTER

Jim Wallace was the Liberal Democrat MP for Orkney and Shetland between 1983 and 2001. He became the MSP for Orkney in 1999, until standing down in 2007. The Leader of the Scottish Liberal Democrats between 1992 and 2005, he was a member of the Scottish Executive between 1999 and 2005 and the Deputy First Minister during the same period. He has been a Peer in the House of Lords since leaving the Scottish Parliament in 2007.

HUMZA YOUSAF, SCOTTISH NATIONAL PARTY

Humza Yousaf was elected as an SNP MSP for the Glasgow Region in 2011, and became a member of the Scottish Government in 2012. In 2016, he won the Glasgow Pollok constituency.

SPCB Staff

JAMES BROWN, ADMINISTRATOR, SOLICITOR'S OFFICE

James Brown joined the Scottish Parliament in 2016 as a Modern Apprentice. He has experienced several offices as an Administrator and, at time of interview, supported the Parliament's Solicitors in the Solicitor's Office.

RUTH CONNELLY, HEAD OF BROADCASTING, BROADCASTING

Ruth Connelly joined the Parliament in 1998, a few months prior to its opening, as the Deputy Head of Broadcasting and Corporate Services. She was tasked with establishing the Broadcasting office for the new Parliament. She remained a key part of the office throughout her carrer, eventually becoming its head. She retired in 2018.

SIR PAUL GRICE, CLERK AND CHIEF EXECUTIVE, OFFICE OF THE CLERK AND CHIEF EXECUTIVE

Paul Grice previously worked for the Department of Transport, the Department of the Environment and as Private Secretary to Virginia Bottomley MP. After joining the Scottish Office in 1992, he became a member of the Constitution Group in May 1997, with responsibility for the Referendum on establishing the Scottish Parliament. Following that, he managed the Scotland Act which established the new constitutional framework. He was appointed Director of Implementation, setting up the parliamentary organisation and associated support systems, prior to being appointed Clerk and Chief Executive in the summer of 1999. As Chief Executive, he leads the Scottish Parliamentary Service which is responsible for delivering all services to the Parliament and its Members, and is the Parliament's principal adviser on procedural and constitutional matters.

WILLIE HEIGH, HEAD OF PROJECT AND PROGRAMME MANAGEMENT, DIGITAL SERVICES GROUP

Willie Heigh initially joined the Parliament in 1999 as a Project Manager for work carried out on its interim accommodation. He later moved over to the Holyrood building project, initially as a consultant and later as a member of Parliament staff, contributing towards the construction of the Parliament building and the move into it. Following the opening of the new building, he was employed by the Parliament as Projects and Best Value Manager. At the time of the interview, he was Head of Project and Programme Management, responsible for maturing the Parliament's approach to project and programme management and providing assurance to senior management on the performance of strategic projects and programmes.

KEN HUGHES, ASSISTANT CHIEF EXECUTIVE, OFFICE OF THE CLERK AND CHIEF EXECUTIVE

Ken Hughes joined the Scottish Parliament from the Scottish Office in 1999. He has supported committee and chamber business activities in various clerking positions and as Head of Committees and Outreach. At the time of the interview, he was a member of Leadership Group as Assistant Chief Executive.

STEPHEN IMRIE, CLERK TEAM LEADER, COMMITTEE OFFICE

Stephen Imrie joined the Scottish Parliament in 1999 from a research and consultancy organisation that involved working with the European Parliament and Commission in Brussels. He has supported committee and chamber business activities in various clerking positions. At the time of the interview, he was Clerk to the Justice Committee.

ALASDAIR MCCALUIM, GAELIC DEVELOPMENT OFFICER, COMMITTEES AND OUTREACH

Alasdair MacCaluim has been involved in supporting and promoting the use of Gaelic in the Scottish Parliament since arriving in 2002.

MARY-ANN MASSON, INTERNAL COMMUNICATIONS MANAGER, OFFICE OF THE CLERK AND CHIEF EXECUTIVE

Mary-Ann Masson joined the Scottish Parliament in 2004, latterly acting as Secretary to the Leadership Group, the Scottish Parliament's senior management board. At the time of the interview, she was Internal Communications Manager.

DAVID MCGILL, ASSISTANT CHIEF EXECUTIVE, OFFICE OF THE CLERK AND CHIEF EXECUTIVE

David McGill joined the Parliament in 1999 as an Assistant Clerk and has held a number of different positions over the course of his long career in the Parliament, mostly involved in parliamentary business-facing roles, eventually attaining the rank of Assistant Chief Executive by the time of the interview.

MURDO MACLEOD, SUB-EDITOR, OFFICIAL REPORT

Murdo MacLeod joined the Parliament in 1998, months before it first convened, and has been involved in Official Report throughout his career, rising to become Sub-Editor at the time of the interview.

DOUGLAS MILLAR, EVENTS MANAGER, EVENTS AND EXHIBITIONS TEAM

Douglas Millar joined the Parliament as an Administrative Assistant in 1999, working in several different offices over his career. After becoming involved in Events, he was the Festival Manager of the Festival of Politics in 2011 and had become Events Manager by the time of the interview.

ANDREW MYLNE, CLERK TEAM LEADER, CHAMBER OFFICE

Andrew Mylne joined the Scottish Parliament in 1999 from the House of Lords where he held the positions of Junior Clerk, Clerk to European Communities Committee (Sub-Committee B) and Clerk in the Public Bill Office. Andrew spent 20 years as a Scottish Parliament Clerk Team Leader which included spells as the Head of Legislation Team and Clerk to various committees. At the time of the interview, he was Head of the Non-Executive Bills Unit, leading the team that provides advice and support to MSPs seeking to introduce Members' or Committee Bills.

JOHN PATERSON, SECURITY PROGRAMME MANAGER, SECURITY OFFICE

John Paterson was involved in the Scottish Parliament building project from its inception in 1997, through his role in the Scottish Office. After becoming a member of Parliament staff in 1999, he remained with the institution beyond the completion of the project, taking on several Project Management roles. At the time of the interview, he was Project Manager in the Facilities Management Office.

SHONA SKAKLE, HEAD OF ENQUIRIES, COMMUNICATIONS AND DIGITAL DEVELOPMENT, SCOTTISH PARLIAMENT INFORMATION CENTRE (SPICe)

Shona Skakle joined the Scottish Parliament in 1999 from the National Library of Scotland. She has held a series of roles within SPICe. At the time of the interview, she was Head of Enquiries.

NEIL STEWART, SENIOR ASSISTANT CLERK, CHAMBER OFFICE

Neil Stewart had a small number of temporary roles within the Parliament over the course of its first two years, before joining as a permanent member of staff in 2001 as an Assistant Clerk. He has been involved in clerking in the Parliament ever since, with the exception of a two-year spell between 2009 and 2011 when he was seconded to the Scotland Office. At the time of the interview, he was Senior Assistant Clerk in the Legislation Team.

BILL THOMSON, FORMER SPCB ASSISTANT CHIEF EXECUTIVE

Bill Thomson was a senior member of staff at the Parliament for much of its history. After working as the Head of the Chamber Office when he first joined the Parliament in 1999, he took charge of the team planning the Parliament's move from its interim accommodation to the Holyrood building in 2004. He was later Director of Clerking and Reporting, Director of Access and Information and Assistant Chief Executive. In 2014 he left the Parliament. However, he retained an involvement with the institution from an outside role after taking up the position of Commissioner for Ethical Standards in Public Life.

Media

KATRINE BUSSEY

Having worked in local newspapers, most notable the *Paisley Daily Express*, Katrine Bussey secured a position at Press Association, where she has reported on the politics of the Scottish Parliament since 2005.

KIRSTEN CAMPBELL

After working as a producer for the BBC at Westminster between 1998 and 1999, witnessing the passing of the Scotland Act, Kirsten Campbell returned to Scotland to become a part the BBC's team at the new Parliament, where she has remained ever since.

COLIN MACKAY

Having had some involvement with political coverage at the BBC in the 1990s, Colin Mackay became a firm fixture at the Scottish Parliament after moving on to take over the political reporting of Scottish Radio Holdings, later renamed Bauer Radio, which consisted of a collection of smaller stations broadcasting around the country. He later moved over to STV, where he continues his work in the Parliament as Holyrood Editor.

ANDREW NICOLL

Beginning his journalistic career with Dundee's DC Thomson publishing house at a young age, Andrew Nicoll began reporting on politics for *The Courier* after the 1992 general election and moved on to *The Scottish Sun* in 1997 as the paper prepared for the coming of devolution. He has remained a feature of the Parliament's press pack ever since.

BRIAN TAYLOR

The BBC's Scottish Political Editor, Brian Taylor began covering politics from the early days of his journalistic career in the late 1970s. After beginning work with the BBC in 1985, he has covered the Scottish Parliament from its birth in 1999 to the present day.

Luath Press Limited

committed to publishing well written books worth reading

LUATH PRESS takes its name from Robert Burns, whose little collie Luath (*Gael.*, swift or nimble) tripped up Jean Armour at a wedding and gave him the chance to speak to the woman who was to be his wife and the abiding love of his life. Burns called one of the 'Twa Dogs' Luath after Cuchullin's hunting dog in Ossian's *Fingal*. Luath Press was established in 1981 in the heart of Burns country, and is now based a few steps up the road from Burns' first lodgings on Edinburgh's Royal Mile. Luath offers you distinctive writing with a hint of unexpected pleasures.

Most bookshops in the UK, the US, Canada, Australia, New Zealand and parts of Europe, either carry our books in stock or can order them for you. To order direct from us, please send a £sterling cheque, postal order, international money order or your credit card details (number, address of cardholder and expiry date) to us at the address below. Please add post and packing as follows: UK – £1.00 per delivery address; overseas surface mail – £2.50 per delivery address; overseas airmail – £3.50 for the first book to each delivery address, plus £1.00 for each additional book by airmail to the same address. If your order is a gift, we will happily enclose your card or message at no extra charge.

Luath Press Limited
543/2 Castlehill
The Royal Mile
Edinburgh EH1 2ND
Scotland
Telephone: +44 (0)131 225 4326 (24 hours)
email: sales@luath. co.uk
Website: www. luath.co.uk